Alone on a W
Vol

William Clark Russell

Alpha Editions

This edition published in 2024

ISBN : 9789366386645

Design and Setting By
Alpha Editions
www.alphaedis.com
Email - info@alphaedis.com

As per information held with us this book is in Public Domain. This book is a reproduction of an important historical work. Alpha Editions uses the best technology to reproduce historical work in the same manner it was first published to preserve its original nature. Any marks or number seen are left intentionally to preserve its true form.

Contents

VOL. 1 ....- 1 -
CHAPTER I PIERTOWN ....- 3 -
CHAPTER II A BOATING TRIP ....- 18 -
CHAPTER III 'WHO AM I?'...................................- 32 -
CHAPTER IV ALPHONSE'S CONJECTURES ....- 46 -
CHAPTER V ON BOARD 'NOTRE DAME' ....- 56 -
CHAPTER VI A TERRIBLE NIGHT......................................- 79 -
CHAPTER VII CAPTAIN FREDERICK LADMORE ....- 91 -
CHAPTER VIII A KIND LITTLE WOMAN ....- 106 -

VOL. 1

CHAPTER I
PIERTOWN

IN the West of England stands a city surrounded by hills. Its streets are wide, its shops fine and plentiful, and there are many handsome and some stately terraces of houses in it. In the heart of the city a gem of ecclesiastical architecture rears its admirable tower, and this fine old structure is known everywhere as the Abbey Church.

How am I to convey to one who has never beheld them the beauties of the scene when viewed from some commanding eminence—say on a rich autumn afternoon whilst the sun paints every object a tender red, and before the shadows have grown long in the valley? Orchards colour the landscape with the dyes of their fruit and leaves. White houses gleam amidst trees and tracts of vegetation. The violet shadow of a cloud floats slowly down some dark green distant slope. In the pastures cattle are feeding, and the noise of the barking of dogs ascends from the river-side. Rows and crescents of buildings hang in clusters upon the hills, blending with the various hues of the country and lending a grace as of nature's own to the scene. The river flows with a red glitter in its breast past meadows and gardens and nestling cottages.

Many roads more or less steep conduct to the several eminences, in the valley of which peacefully stands this western city. One of them in a somewhat gentle acclivity winds eastwards, and as the wayfarer proceeds along this road he passes through a long avenue of chestnuts, which in the heat of the summer cast a delicious shade upon the dust, and here the air is so pure that it acts upon the spirits like a cordial. The ocean is not very many miles distant, and you taste the saltness of its breath in the summer breeze as it blows down the hillsides, bringing with it a hundred perfumes, and a hundred musical sounds from the orchards and the gardens.

About a mile beyond this avenue of chestnuts there stood—I say there stood, but I do not doubt there still stands—a pretty house of a modern character, such as would be offered for letting or for selling as a 'villa residence.' I will speak of it as of a thing that is past. It was situated on the edge of the hill; on one side the white road wound by it; on the other side its land of about one acre and a half sloped into meadows and pastures, and this wide space of fields sank treeless, defined by hedges, well stocked in the seasons with sheep and cows and other cattle, to the silver line of the river.

Now have I brought you to my home, to the home in which I was living a little while before the strange and terrible experience that, with the help of another pen, I am about to relate befel me. And that you may thoroughly understand the story which I shall almost immediately enter upon, it is necessary that I should submit a little home picture to you.

It was a Sunday afternoon early in the month of October in a year that is all too recent for the endurance of memory. A party of four, of which one was a little boy aged two, were seated at table drinking tea in the dining-room of the house, which stood a mile beyond the chestnut avenue. Upon the hearth-rug, where was stretched a soft white blanket, lay a baby of eight months old, tossing its fat pink legs and dragging at the tube of a feeding-bottle. A lady sat at the head of the table.

This lady was in her twenty-sixth year—no one better knew the date of her birth than I. She was a handsome woman, and presently you will understand why I exhibit no reluctance in speaking of her beauty. I will be brief in my description of her, but I will invite your attention to a sketch that, in its relations to this tale, carries, as you will discover, a deeper significance than ordinarily accompanies the portraits of the heroes or heroines of romance.

She was in her twenty-sixth year, I say. Her hair was dark, not black. I am unable to find a name for its peculiar shade. It was so abundant as to be inconvenient to its owner, whose character was somewhat impatient, so that every morning's wrestle with the long thick tresses was felt as a trouble and often as a cause of vexatious delay. Her eyebrows were thick and arched, and, as she wore her hair low, but a very little of her white well-shaped brow was to be seen. Her nose was after the Roman type, but not too large nor prominent, yet it gave her an air as though she held her head high, and it also communicated an expression of eagerness to the whole countenance. Her complexion was a delicate bloom, her mouth was small, the teeth very white and regular. She had a good figure, a little above the medium height of women, with a promise in her shape of stoutness when her years should have increased. She was simply dressed, and wore but little jewellery, no more than a thin watch-chain round her neck and a wedding-ring and two other rings on the same finger.

Such was the lady in her twenty-sixth year who sat at the head of the tea-table on that October Sunday afternoon.

At her side was her little boy, two years old. He was a beautiful child with golden hair and dark blue eyes. He sat in a high child's chair on his mother's left, and whilst he waited for her to feed him he beat the table with a spoon.

At the table on the right sat the husband of this lady, a man entering upon his thirty-first year. He was tall, thin, and fair, and wore small whiskers, and his eyes were a dark grey. Handsome he was not, but he had a well-bred air, and his face expressed a gentle and amiable nature.

Confronting the lady at the head of the table was her twin sister. Nearly always between twins there is a strong family likeness. I have heard of twins who resembled each other so closely as to be mistaken one for the other unless they were together, when, to be sure, there must be some subtle difference to distinguish them. There was undoubtedly a family likeness between these two sisters, but it appeared rather in their smile and in certain small tricks of posture and of gesture, and in their walk and in the attitudes which they insensibly fell into when seated; in these things lay a family likeness rather than in their faces. Their voices did not in the least resemble each other's. That of the lady who sat at the head of the table was somewhat high-pitched; her accents were delivered with impulse and energy, no matter how trivial might be the subject on which she discoursed. Her sister, on the other hand, had a sweet, low, musical voice; she pronounced her words with a charming note of plaintiveness, and she never spoke much at a time nor often. Her hair was not so plentiful as her sister's; it was a light bright brown, with a gloss upon it like that of the shell of a horse-chestnut, but it had not the rich deep dye of that nut. She wore it with a simplicity that was infinitely becoming to her beauty. Beautiful she was, far more so than her sister; hers was a beauty far more tender and womanly than her sister's; you thought of the meekness and the sweetness of the dove in looking at her, and the expression of her dark-brown eyes was dove-like. She was shorter than her sister, but equally well shaped, and she was the younger.

These four sitting at table, and the little baby of eight months tossing its tiny toes shod with knitted shoes upon a blanket on the hearth-rug, formed the occupants of that parlour, and were the living details of the domestic picture that the curtain of the terrible drama of my life rises upon. The rays of the westering sun streamed upon the windows of the room, and the atmosphere was warm with crimson light. One window stood open, but the church bells had not yet begun to ring for evening service, and the peace of the English Sabbath lay upon the land outside: a peace scarcely disturbed by the distant barking of dogs, by the occasional moaning lowing of near cattle, and by the drowsy murmuring hum of bees and flies amongst the flowers under the windows.

Who were these people, and what was their name? The name of the gentleman was John Campbell, and the lady seated at the head of the table was his wife, Agnes—Agnes Campbell, whose story she herself now relates, and the sweet sister at the foot of the table was Mary Hutchinson.

I had been married at the time when my story opens a little above three years. My father was Colonel Hutchinson, of the Honourable East India Company's service. He had distinguished himself in India in a period of terrible peril, but he had died before he could reap the reward of his valour and his judgment. He died a poor man, his whole fortune amounting to no more than five thousand pounds; but the pension my mother drew, conjointly with the interest of my father's little fortune, enabled her to live in tolerable comfort, and after my father's death we took up our abode in the noble old city of Bath, where we dwelt happily, making many friends and enjoying a round of simple pleasures.

Society in Bath is largely, almost wholly, composed of ladies; young men are scarce, and marriage at the best is but vaguely dreamed of, though hope is sufficiently constant to support the spirits.

It chanced that Mary and I were invited one evening to play a round game of cards at the house of a friend. We went, expecting to find the company formed entirely of girls like ourselves, with perhaps one or two old fogeys. But soon after our arrival a gentleman was shown into the room, and introduced to us as Mr. John Campbell. He was the only young man present; the other gentlemen were composed of a general, a colonel, and an admiral, whose united ages I afterwards calculated would have exactly amounted to two hundred years. I did not notice that Mr. Campbell paid me much attention that evening. Mary afterwards said he seldom had his eyes off me, but *that* I did not observe. On the contrary, I thought he looked very often and very admiringly at *her*.

Well, he saw us to the door of our house, to use the homely phrase, and on the following afternoon he called upon us; but if it was love at first sight on his part, I cannot say that he illustrated his fervour by his behaviour. He was very polite, very kind, very attentive; seemed happy in my society, was a frequent visitor at our house, would steal an hour from business to find himself an excuse to meet us in the gardens or park where we walked; but that was all.

If I had been led by the reading of novels to suppose that a man looks love when he means love, I might have searched Mr. Campbell's face in vain for any expression of deep-seated sentiment. Indeed, after three months, I could not have said that he was more in love with me than with my sister. But by the end of that time I must own that I was very much in love with him. And though so tenderly did I love my sister that I would gladly have relinquished him to her, had her love for him been as mine, yet to no other woman could I have parted with him without the belief—which to be sure I used to laugh at after I was married—that my heart would break if he did not make me his. But my heart was not to be broken because of his not loving me and making me his, for within six months from the date of our meeting we were married, and I was the happiest girl in all England, and my sister as happy as I in my happiness.

My husband was a solicitor. His practice in those days was small and would not have supported him even as a bachelor; but he had been the only son of a man who was able to leave him an income of several hundreds a year. We went abroad for a month, and I returned to find my poor mother dead. This loss left my sister without a relative in the world saving myself. It is seldom that this can be said of man or woman. To be without a relative in this complicated world of aunts and uncles, of nieces and nephews, and of cousins no matter how far removed, seems incredible. There may be plenty of people who are alone in the sense of not knowing who their relatives are, though they would find they had relations in plenty were they to seek them or were they to come into a fortune; but it is rare indeed to hear of anyone who out of his or her perfect knowledge of the family connections can positively assert, 'I have not a relative in the world.'

Yet thus it was with my sister and me when my mother died. But I will not delay my story to explain how this happened. Therefore, being alone in the world, my sister came to live with my husband and me. How greatly her making one of us added to my happiness I cannot express. I will not pretend that it did grieve me to leave my poor mother: no, nature works forwards; the fruit falls from the tree, the young bird flutters from its nest; it is nature's law that a child should part from its parent, and deep as the sadness of separation may seem at the time, it will show but as a light-hearted grief at the best when looked back upon and contrasted with other sorrows of life.

But it was a bitter pain to me to part with my sister. We had grown up side by side; we were as blossoms upon one stalk, and the sap of the single stalk fed the two flowers.

And now as we sat drinking tea in the parlour of our house on that fine October Sunday afternoon, our conversation was as homely as the picture we made. Nevertheless it involved a topic of considerable interest to us. My little boy Johnny had been looking somewhat pale, and his appetite was not as I, his mother, considered it should be. The summer had been a very hot one, and when it is even moderately warm in most parts of England, it is commonly very broiling indeed in our city of the Abbey Church, where there are tall hills to protect the population from the breeze, where the roads are steep, glaring, and dusty, and where the width of many of the streets is quite out of proportion to the stature of the houses, so that you do not know where to look for shade.

My husband's business would not suffer him to leave home until the early autumn, and he could not prevail upon me to go away without him; but now he was able to take a holiday for a month, and the doctor had recommended the seaside for little Johnny and the baby, and as we sat drinking tea we talked of the best place to go to.

'It does not matter to me what part of the coast you choose,' said my husband. 'I only stipulate that you shall not select a town that is confidently recommended by the whole of the medical faculty, and whose medical officer every year sends to the newspapers a statement that the death-rate is the lowest in England, and that it is the healthiest seaside resort in the United Kingdom.'

'Then you shut every seaside town against us,' said my sister, 'for every seaside town is the healthiest in England.'

I named Margate; my husband made a grimace.

'No,' he exclaimed, 'I should not like to return to Bath and say we have been to Margate. It was only the other day I heard General Cramp swear that Margate was not the vulgarest place in all England, oh no! but the vulgarest place in all the world.'

'Its air is very fine,' said I, 'and it is fine air that we want.' And here I looked at Johnny. 'What does it matter to us what sort of people go to Margate, if its air is good?'

'I will not go to Margate,' said my husband.

My sister named two or three towns on the coast.

'Let us,' said my husband, 'go to some place where there is no hotel and where there is no pier.'

'And where there is no circulating library,' cried I, 'and where there are two miles of mud when the water is out.'

And then I named several towns as my sister had, but my suggestions were not regarded. At this point baby began to roar, and my husband rose to ring for the nurse, but it was nurse's 'Sunday out,' and Mary and I were taking her place. Mary picked baby up off the blanket, and holding its cheek to hers, sung softly to it in her low sweet voice. The darling was instantly silent. The effect of my sister's plaintive melodious voice upon fretful children was magical. I remember once calling with her upon a lady who wished that we should see her baby. The baby was brought into the room, and the moment it saw us it began to yell. My sister stepped up to it as it sat on the nurse's arm, and looking at it in the face with a smile began to sing, and the infant, silencing its cries, stared back at her with its mouth wide open in the very posture of a scream, but as silent as though it had been a doll. When she ceased to sing and turned from it, it roared again, and again she silenced it by singing.

My baby lay hushed in her arms, and the sweet eyes of Mary looked at us over the little fat cheek that she nestled to her throat, and we continued to discourse upon the best place to go to.

My husband named a small seaside town, and I could see by the expression of his face he meant that we should go there. It was many years since he had visited it, but he recollected and described the beauties of the scenery of the coast with enthusiasm. It was on the Bristol Channel, at no very considerable distance from the city in which we dwelt, and he said he wished to go there because, should there come a call upon him from the office, he would be able to make the double journey, with plenty of leisure between for all he might have to do, in a day, computing that day from eight till midnight.

'Oh! it is a beautiful romantic spot, Agnes,' said he. 'Its sands, when the water is out, are as firm as this floor. It has high, dark cliffs, magnificently bold and rugged, and when the breaker bursts upon the sand, the cliffs echo its voice, and you seem to hear the note of an approaching tempest.'

'But it is a cheerful place, John? Cliffs and sands are very well, but in a month one wearies of cliffs and sands, and in a month again how many days of wet will there be?'

'It is cheerful—very,' said my husband. 'Its cheerfulness is inborn, like good-nature in a man. It owes nothing of its brightness to excursionists, to steamboats, to Punch and Judy, and to German bands. It has three good streets and a number of clean lodging-houses.'

'Has it a pier and a hotel?' asked Mary.

'It has what the cockneys call a jetty,' answered my husband. 'I should prefer to term it a pier. What is the difference between a pier and a jetty? This jetty is short, massive, very richly tarred, and just the sort of jetty for Johnny to fall over the edge of if he is not looked after. There is a wooden canopy at the extremity of it under which, Mary, you will be able to sit and read your favourite poet without risk of being intruded upon. The verses of your favourite poet will be set to music by the rippling of the water among the massive supports of the pier, and you will have nothing to do but to be happy.'

'Are there any boats?' I asked.

'Many capital boats,' he answered.

'Sailing boats?' said I.

'Sailing boats and rowing boats,' said he.

'I shall often want to go out sailing,' said I. 'What is more heavenly than sailing?'

'You will have to go alone so far as I am concerned, Agnes,' said Mary.

'Yes, but John will often accompany me,' said I.

'Not very often,' he exclaimed. 'Had I been a lover of sailing I should have gone to sea, instead of which I am a solicitor, and I spell sails with an "e" and not with an "i." Well, is it settled?' he continued, drawing a pipe case from his pocket and extracting the pipe from it. 'I believe there will be time for half a pipe of tobacco before we go to church.'

But the nurse being out I could not go to church, and my sister would not leave me alone with the children, and my husband, instead of filling half a pipe filled a whole one, and took no heed of the church bells when their happy peaceful chimes floated through the open window. Indeed it was *not* settled; the subject was too interesting to be swiftly dismissed, yet my husband had his way in the end, as usually happened, for before evening service was over we had arranged to spend a month at the little town whose praises he had sung so poetically.

Next day he made a journey to the shores of the Bristol Channel to seek for lodgings. But the accommodation he required was not to be found in apartments, and when he returned he told me that he had taken a house standing near the edge of the cliff in a garden of its own. A few days later our little family proceeded to the sea coast. We left two servants behind us to look after the house, and the only domestic we took with us was the nurse, a person of about my own age, who had been with me at this time about six weeks, having replaced an excellent, trustworthy young woman who had left me to get married.

I will call the little place from which dates the story of my terrific experiences, Piertown.

What with having to change here, and to get out there, and to wait somewhere else, the journey was a tedious one, and when we arrived it was raining hard and blowing very strong, and I remember as we drove from the railway station catching sight through the streaming window glass of the white waves of the sea rushing like bodies of snow out of the pale haze of the rain and the spray, and I also remember that I heard a strange low voice of thunder in the air, made by the huge breakers as they tumbled in hills of water upon the beach and rushed backwards into the sea in sheets of froth.

It was so cold that we were very glad to find a cheerful fire in the parlour, that was rendered yet more hospitable to the sight by the table being equipped for a two o'clock dinner. The house was small, but very strongly built, with thick plate-glass windows in the lower rooms, against which the wind and the rain were hissing as though an engine were letting off steam close by. A couple of maid-servants had been left in the house. Never could I have imagined that servants would be willing to sleep as those two did in one small bed, in a tiny garret where all the light they had fell through a skylight window about the size of a book. But I have noticed in the country, that is to say, in rural parts and quiet towns such as Piertown, servants are grateful and dutiful for such food and lodging as would cause them to be incessantly grumbling and changing their places in cities like Bath.

Baby and little Johnny were taken upstairs by the nurse, and my husband and Mary and I went to the window and stood gazing at the sea. We had a very clear view of it. The house stood within a few yards of the edge of the cliff, and the extremity of the garden between was bounded by a dwarf wall of flint which left the prospect open.

'What do you think of that sight, Agnes?' said my husband. 'Would sailing be heavenly to-day, do you think?'

'Never more heavenly if one could feel safe,' said I. 'How swiftly a boat would rush before such a wind as this! Hark to the roaring in the chimney! It makes me feel as if I were in the cabin of a ship. It is delightful. It is like being at sea and enjoying the full spirit of it without suffering the horrors of being tossed and bruised, and without any chance of being upset and shipwrecked.'

'You should have married a sailor,' said my husband dryly.

'What have you been reading lately, Agnes, to put this sudden love of the sea into your head?' said Mary. 'You used not to care for the water.'

'I have been reading nothing to make me love the sea,' I answered; 'but when I look at such a sight as that I feel that if I were a man I should consider that the earth was formed of something more than land, and that the best part of it is not where trees grow and where houses are built.'

My husband laughed. 'One hour of *that* would cure you,' said he pointing. 'One *hour*, indeed! Ten minutes of it. I tell you what—there is a very heavy sea running to-day. It *must* be so, for we are high-perched here, and look how defined are the shapes of the waves as they come storming out of the mist towards the land.'

'I wish a ship would pass,' said I. 'I should like to see her roll and plunge.'

And for some time after my husband and Mary had withdrawn from the window I stood gazing at the bleared and throbbing scene of ocean, hoping and longing to see a ship go by, little suspecting that my wishes were as wicked as though they were those of a wrecker, for had any ship been close enough in to the coast to enable me to see her amid the thickness that was upon the face of the streaming and rushing waters, nothing could have saved her from being driven ashore, where in all probability her crew would have perished.

But in the afternoon the weather cleared; it continued to blow a strong wind right upon the land, but the sky opened into many blue lakes, and changed into a magnificent picture of immense bodies of stately sailing cream-coloured cloud, upon which the setting sun shone, colouring their skirts with a dark rich gold, and the horizon expanded to as far as the eye could pierce, with one staggering and leaning shaft of white upon the very rim of the sea.

'Let us go and look at the town,' said my husband; and Mary and I put on our hats and jackets and the three of us sallied forth.

We had to walk some distance to reach the little town, and when we arrived there was not very much to see. The three streets were neither spacious nor splendid; on the contrary, they struck me as rather mean and weather-beaten. But then people do not leave cities in order to view the shops and streets of little seaside towns. Piertown lay in a sort of chasm. It was as though a party of fishermen in ancient days, wandering along the coast in search of a good site for the erection of their cottages, and falling in with this great split in the cliff, as though an earthquake had not long before happened, had exclaimed, 'Let us settle here.' There was a peculiar smell of salt in the streets, and the roadways and pavements presented a sort of faint sparkling surface, as though a great deal of brine had fallen upon them and dried up. There was also a smell of kippered herring in the strong wind, and it seemed to proceed from every shop door that we passed.

Very few people were to be seen. We were much stared at by the shopmen through their windows, and here and there a little knot of lounging men dressed as boatmen hushed their hoarse voices to intently gaze at us.

'This is what I like,' said my husband. 'Here is all the privacy that we could desire, and the most delightful primitiveness also. A professional man when he takes a holiday ought to give crowded places a very wide berth, and put himself as close to nature—to nature, rugged, homely and roaring, after this pattern,' said he with a sweep of his hand, 'as his requirements of eating and drinking and sleeping will permit.'

'It seems a very dull place,' said I when, having reached the top of one of the three steep streets, we turned to retrace our steps. 'If the weather does not allow me to have plenty of boating I shall soon wish myself home again.'

'You will not find a circulating library here,' said Mary, looking around her. 'I should not suppose that many people belonging to Piertown are able to read.'

'The place is made up of grocers' shops,' said my husband. 'What a queer smell of bloaters!'

I amused myself by counting no less than five grocers' shops in one street, and I did not see a single person resembling a customer in any one of them. I pulled my husband's arm to stop him opposite a shop in whose windows I believed I saw three men hanging by the neck. They proved to be complete suits of oilskins, each surmounted by one of those nautical helmets called sou'-westers, and at a little distance, as they dangled in the twilight within the windows, they exactly resembled three mariners who had committed suicide.

We now walked down to the pier, and there the great plain of the ocean stretched before us without the dimmest break of land anywhere along its confines, and the white surf boiled within the toss of a pebble from us. The pier projected from a short esplanade; along this esplanade ran a terrace of mean stunted structures, eight in all; and my husband, after looking and counting, exclaimed: 'Five of them are public-houses. Yes! this is the seaside.'

The pier forked straight out for a short distance, then rounded sharply to the right, thus forming a little harbour, in the shelter of which lay a cluster of boats of several kinds. The massive piles and supports of the pier broke the weight of the seas, which rushed hissing white as milk amongst the black timbers; but the water within was considerably agitated nevertheless, and the boats hopped and plunged and jumped and rubbed their sides one against another, straining at the ropes which held them, as though they were timid living creatures like sheep, terrified by the noise and appearance of the waters, and desperately struggling at their tethers in their desire to get on shore.

We stood looking, inhaling deeply and with delight the salt sweetness of the strong ocean breeze. The land soared on either hand from the little town, and ran away in dark masses of towering cliff, and far as the eye could follow went the white line of the surf, with a broad platform of grey hard sand betwixt it and the base of the cliff. Here and there in one or another of the public-house windows glimmered a face whose eyes surveyed us steadfastly. We might make sure by the manner in which we were looked at, that Piertown was not greatly troubled by visitors.

There was a wooden post near the entrance of the pier, and upon it leaned the figure of a man clad in trousers of a stuff resembling blanket, a rusty coat buttoned up to his neck, around which was a large shawl, and upon his head he wore a yellow sou'-wester. He might have been carved out of wood, so motionless was his posture and so intent his gaze at the horizon, where there was nothing to be seen but water, though I strained my sight in the hope of perceiving the object which appeared to fascinate him. A short clay pipe, of the colour of soot, projected from his lips. He seemed to hold it thus as one might wear an ornament, for no smoke issued from it.

We drew close, and my husband said: 'Good afternoon.'

The man looked slowly round, surveyed us one after another, then readjusting himself upon his post and fastening his eyes afresh upon the horizon, he responded in a deep voice: 'Good arternoon.'

'Is there anything in sight?' said my husband.

'No,' answered the man.

'Then what are you looking at?'

'I ain't looking,' answered the man; 'I'm a-thinking.'

'And what are you thinking of?'

'Why,' said the man, 'I'm a-thinking that I han't tasted a drop o' beer for two days.'

'This, indeed, is being at the seaside,' said my husband cheerfully, and putting his hand in his pocket he produced a sixpence, which he gave to the man.

The effect was remarkable; the man instantly stood upright, and went round to the other side of the post to lean over it, so that he might confront us. And it was remarkable in other ways; for no sooner had my husband given the man the sixpence than the doors of two or three of the public-houses opposite opened, and several figures dressed like this man emerged and approached us very slowly, halting often and looking much at the weather, and then approaching us by another step, and all in a manner as though they were acting unconsciously, and without the least idea whatever that my husband had given the man some money.

He was a man of about forty-five or fifty years of age, with a very honest cast of countenance, the expression of which slightly inclined towards surliness. You will wonder that I should take such particular notice of a mere lounging boatman; and yet this same plain, common-looking sailor, was to become the most memorable of all the persons I had ever met with in my life.

CHAPTER II
A BOATING TRIP

It was not yet evening, but the sun was very low in the west on our right hand; a large moon would be rising a little while before eight; the breeze continued to blow strong, and the ocean rolled into the land in tall dark-green lines of waves, melting as they charged in endless succession into wide spaces of foam, orange coloured by the sunset.

'Do you hear that echo of thunder in the cliff I told you about?' said my husband.

I listened and said 'Yes.'

'It is like a distant firing of guns,' said Mary.

'You have some good boats down there dancing beside the pier,' said my husband to the boatman.

'Ay,' answered the boatman, 'you'll need to sail a long way round the coast to find better boats than them.'

'That is a pretty boat, Mary,' said I, pointing to one with two masts—a tall mast in the fore-part and a short mast at the stern; she was painted green and red, and she was very clean and white inside, and she appeared in my eyes the prettiest of all the boats as she dived and tumbled and leaped buoyantly and not without grace upon the sharp edges of the broken water.

'That's my boat, lady,' said the sailor.

'What is her name?' inquired Mary.

'The *Mary Hann*, he answered. 'I named her after my wife. My wife is gone dead. I've got no wife now but she,' and he pointed with his thumb backwards at his boat, 'and she's but a poor wife too. She airns little enough for me. T'other kept the home together with taking in washing, but nobody comes to Piertown now. Folks want what's called attractions. But the Local Board'll do nothen except buy land as belongs to the men who forms the Local Board, and the likes of me has to pay for that there land, and when it's bought fower five times as much as it's worth, it's left waste. Lord, the jobbery! Are you making any stay here, sir?'

'Yes,' answered my husband, 'we are here for a month.'

'And when might ye have arrived?' inquired the boatman.

'To-day,' replied my husband.

'There's some very good fishing to be had here, sir,' said the boatman. 'If I may make so bold, whenever you wants a trip out, whether for fishing or rowing or sailing, if so be as you'll ask for me, my name being William Hitchens, best known as Bill Hitchens, pronounced in one word Billitchens—for there's parties here as'll swear they didn't know who you vos asking for if you don't call me Billitchens—if you ever want a boat, sir, and you ladies, if you'll ask for Billitchens, you'll meet with satisfaction. There's nothen to touch the *Mary Hann* in sailing, whilst for fishing she's as steady as a rock, as you may guess, sir, by obsarving her beam.'

'When I want a boat I will ask for Billitchens,' said my husband, glancing at me with a smile in his eye. 'This lady—my wife—is fonder of the sea than I am. I dare say she will sometimes take a cruise with you. But the weather must be fine when she does so.'

'You trust the weather to me, lady,' said the boatman. 'Man and boy for over forty-eight year I've been a-crawling about this beach and a-studying the weather. You leave him to me. Whenever you want a cruise you ask for Billitchens and the *Mary Hann*, and if the weather ain't promising for the likes of such a lady as you, you shall have the truth.'

'What are your charges?' said my husband.

'Wan and sixpence an hour,' answered the boatman cheerfully, 'but if you'd like to engage my boat by the week ye shall have her at your own price, giving me so much every time ye takes me along.'

'Is she not heavy to row?' said I.

'Lord love ye!' he cried, gazing at his boat with a sour smile of wonder at the question. 'A hinfant could send her spinning. 'Sides,' he added, 'I'll take care to ship a pair o' light oars for you, lady, what's called sculls, nigh as light as this here baccay-pipe.'

'Well, good afternoon, Mr. Hitchens,' said my husband, and we strolled in the direction of our home, for the shadow of the evening was now upon the sea, and the strong wind seemed to have grown very cold on a sudden.

However, before we retired to rest the night fell silent, the sea stretched in a dark sheet, and from our windows, so high seated was the house, the ocean looked to slope steep into the sky, as though, indeed, it were the side of a mighty hill. The moon rode over it, and under the orb lay a column of glorious silver which stirred like the coils of a moving serpent as the swell or the heave of the water ran through it. The dark body of a ship passed through that brilliant path of light as we stood looking, and the sight was beautiful.

My little ones were sleeping well. Johnny slept in our room and the baby with the nurse, for my husband could not bear to be disturbed in his sleep. I looked at my boy, and asked my husband to tell me if he did not think there was already a little bloom on Johnny's cheek, and I kissed my child's sweet brow and golden hair.

But it was long before my eyes closed in sleep. I lay hearkening to the dull subdued thunder of the surf beating upon the beach far below at the foot of the cliffs. It was a new strange noise to me, and I lay listening to it as though to a voice muttering in giant whispers out of the hush of midnight; and when at last I fell asleep I dreamt that I was in the *Mary Hann*, and that Bill Hitchens was steering the boat, and that she was sailing directly up the line of glorious silver under the moon; and I remember that I asked him in my dream how long it would take to reach the moon that as we sailed waxed bigger and soared higher; but instead of answering he put his knuckles into his eyes and began to sob and cry, and I awoke to hear little Johnny calling to me to take him into my bed.

And now followed days as happy as light hearts and bright skies and good health could render them. The weather continued splendid. Sometimes it was as hot as ever it had been during the month of July in the city of the Abbey Church. There was a pleasant neighbourhood, a country of woods and verdant dingles and swelling pastures, and we made many excursions, and in particular did we enjoy a visit to some old ruins which had once been an abbey, but now its windows yawned, its roof was gone, large portions of masonry had fallen, its floor was a tangled growth of rank grass and weeds. We listened to the wind whistling through these ruins: we listened with bated breath and with raised imaginations, for the noise of the wind was like the chanting of friars intermixed with a thin wailing of women's voices; and as I listened I could not help thinking to myself that it was as though the ghosts of long-departed monks and chaste and holy nuns had viewlessly assembled round about us to sing some solemn dirge, and that if our eyes were as fine a sense as our hearing—if, indeed, we could *see* the invisible as we could *hear* it—we might behold the vision of the building itself spread over our heads and on either hand of us, in roof, in glorious coloured window, in sepulchral monument.

Here it was that my little Johnny, in running from me towards the grass which grew upon what had been the pavement of this ancient abbey, tripped and fell and lay screaming as though fearfully hurt. Mary took him up: he was not hurt. My husband, looking into the grass to observe what had tripped the child, put his hand upon something grey and picked up a little skull. 'Good God!' he cried, casting it from him with a shudder, 'let us get away from this place.' But Mary remained behind alone for some minutes, with her eyes bent upon the little skull, musing upon it.

Though we made several inland excursions our chief haunts were the pier and the beach. Those were happy days indeed. My sister and I would take camp-stools down on to the sands, and long mornings did we thus pass, my husband moving indolently here and there, smoking, examining pools of water, stooping to pick up a shell; Johnny scooping with a stick at my side; baby sleeping in the arms of the nurse. There we would sit and watch the quiet surface of the sea that melted into the blue air where the sky came down to it, and gaze at the oncoming breaker poising its tall emerald-green head for a breathless instant, like some huge snake about to strike, ere tumbling in thunder and snow and roaring seawards in a cataract of yeast.

We seemed—indeed, I believe we were—the only visitors in the place. Nobody intruded upon us; the miles of sand were our own. Robinson Crusoe's dominion was not more uninterrupted.

The boatman named William Hitchens had called twice at the house early in the morning to know if we would go for a nice little sail or row during the day, but the answer I had sent by the servant was, 'Not yet.' I was in no hurry to go for a nice little sail or a row. When I was on the sands the sea was so close to me that it was almost the same as being on it; and the novelty of having the sea feathering to my feet in white and broken waters remained too great an enjoyment for some days to induce a wish in me for wider experiences. And then again, neither Mary nor my husband had the least taste for boating, so that if I went I must go alone. I was not even able to have my children with me, for the nurse declared that the mere looking from the beach at a boat rocking upon the water made her feel ill, and I dared not single-handed take the children, for how could I, holding the baby, have looked after little Johnny, who was always on the move, crawling here and creeping there, and who was just the sort of child to wriggle on to a seat of the boat and tumble overboard whilst my head was turned?

However, after we had been at Piertown five days we walked down to the sands as usual after breakfast, and as we passed the entrance of the pier Bill Hitchens approached us, pulling at a grey lock of hair that hung upon his forehead under an old felt bandit-shaped hat.

'A beautiful morning for a sail or a row, lady,' said he, addressing himself to me as though he had long before made up his mind that there was no custom to be got out of my husband and my sister, 'why not wenture on an hour, mum? There's as pretty a little offshore wind a-blowing as could be wished. And look how smooth the water is! Only let me draw you clear of this here ground swell, and ye won't know you're afloat. Or if you don't like sailing, I'll put a small oar into the boat, and with me rowing agin ye, lady, ye shall see how light a boat she is.'

'Go, Agnes,' said my husband, observing that I looked wistfully at the water.

'Come, Mary!' said I.

'No, dear,' she answered, 'I am certain to suffer from headache afterwards.'

'Why don't *you* come along, sir?' said the boatman to my husband.

'Because I am very well, thank you, Billitchens, and I wish to remain well,' answered my husband.

'I will go,' said I, and instantly the boatman was in motion. He ran with uncouth gestures to a ladder that descended the pierside, disappeared down it, and presently emerged in a little skiff which he propelled with an oar over the stern. Having arrived at his boat, which was moored in the middle of the small harbour, if I may so term the space of water within the embrace of the crooked arm of the pier, he freed and brought her to some steps. I entered, perhaps a little nervously, sat down, and Bill Hitchens throwing his oars over pulled the boat out to sea. Little Johnny screamed and wept, imagining that I was leaving him for ever. I kissed my hand and waved it to him, and Mary, taking the little fellow in her arms, comforted him.

Now out of that simple English scene of coast life, out of the familiar commonplace experience of a boating trip, what, if it were not death, what should be able to shape itself so potent in all horror as to utterly and absolutely shipwreck my happiness and make a frightful tragedy of my life? Death it might well have been; again and again small sailing boats are capsizing and their inmates are thrown into the water and drowned; but worse than death was to befal me. When I close my eyes and behold with the vision of my mind the scene of that little town, and the terraces of the cliffs, though I am able to connect the long chain of circumstance link by link, the memory of the disaster and all that followed the disaster affects me even at this instant of time with the violence of a paralysing revelation. I know the past to be true, and still I gaze dumbly and with terror backwards, incapable of crediting it.

But the dreadful misfortune that was to overwhelm me did not happen at once. No: my short excursion that morning I thoroughly enjoyed. All was safe, well, and delightful. I told the boatman to keep somewhat close in to the shore, and I held my husband and sister and children in view all the while. The boatman rowed leisurely, and my dear ones on the shore kept pace with the boat until they had arrived at their favourite spot on the sands, where they seated themselves and watched me. I rowed a little and found the oar the man had placed in the boat for my use very light and manageable; but I plied it unskilfully; indeed I was but a wretched oarswoman. Yet it amused me to dip the blade into the water however clumsily, and to feel that the boat received something of her impulse from the swing of my figure.

Bill Hitchens talked much, and had I heeded his conversation I might have found his queer words and odd thoughts and expressions amusing; but I was too much occupied with my oar, and with looking at the group on the sands, and with admiring the coast, to attend to his queer speech. And, indeed, we were at just such a distance from the coast as enabled me to witness in perfection its incomparable romantic beauties. The cliffs rose in dark and rugged ramparts, and their gloomy massy colours were peculiarly defined by the line of white surf which, the fall of the breakers being continuous, seemed fixed as though painted along the foot of the coast. The windows of the house we occupied sparkled over the edge of the heights, but the structure was so high lodged, the altitude from the sea appeared so prodigious, that spite of the softening shadow of trees behind it, and spite of its quaint and cosy shape, it had an odd, wild, windy look to my eyes, and I wondered as I gazed at it that it had not been levelled long ago by one of the many hurricanes of wind which Bill Hitchens told me thundered across the sea and against the land in winter time, blind with snow and black with flying scud. And the town made me think of Tennyson's description of a coastal village, for there was a frosty sparkle upon the houses as though they were formed of blocks of rock salt. The sky was a deep blue, and I noticed that it seemed to tremble and thrill where the bend of it disappeared past the edge of the cliffs, as if the dye of the cliffs themselves were lifting and sifting into it, and deepening the beauty of its hue just there. The water was everywhere flashful with the light wind that was blowing from the land. Presently the boatman said:

'Lady, let me gi' you a bit of a sail?'

I consented, and he took my oar from me and laid it in the boat, then loosed a big sail that lay upon the seats and hoisted it, and afterwards he set a little sail at the stern, and then sat down at the tiller and steered, making the boat skim along on a line with the beach. My dear ones flourished their hands to me.

This was enjoyment indeed. The boat seemed to me to sail wonderfully fast; I looked over the stern and perceived that she left behind her a long furrow as beautiful with its ornamentation of foam and bubble and eddies as a length of rich lace. Hitchens sailed the boat to and fro, and all the time he was bidding me observe what a beautiful boat she was, how there was nothing whatever to be afraid of, how in such a boat as the *Mary Hann*, as he called her, a party of people might sail round the United Kingdom in perfect comfort and security.

'Only make it worth my while,' said he, 'and I'd go to Ameriky in this here boat. Make it worth my while, lady, and I'd double the Harn in her. Ameriky was discovered by folks as would have swopped their precious eyes for such a boat as this here to make the voyage in. I don't speak of Australey, for Cook he had a ship; but I've heered tell of Columbus; there's one of us chaps as has read all about that gent and is always a-yarning about him; and ower and ower I've heard him say that that there Columbus would have swopped his precious eyes for the likes of such a boat as the *Mary Hann* for to make his discovery with.'

In this manner Bill Hitchens discoursed about his boat, as he sat beside the tiller with his head well between his shoulders and his back rounded like a cat's at the sight of a dog.

After this I was continually making excursions with Bill Hitchens. Having got to know him, I never would hire another in his place. Indeed, he took care that nobody should supplant him, and called for orders every morning with the punctuality of the butcher or the grocer. Often I would go out twice a day, so keen was my enjoyment of the pastime of sailing and rowing. Twice my husband accompanied me, but after the second time he told me he had had enough, and he went no more in the boat. Once I coaxed Mary into joining me, and in less than five minutes the boatman was obliged to put her ashore, and when I returned two hours later I found her motionless on the sofa with a sick headache.

The behaviour of the boatman did not belie the character I seemed to find written in his face. He proved a very honest, civil, deserving fellow, possessed of a quality of sourness that imparted a particular relish to his odd manner of speaking. I did not fear to be alone with this man. I had every confidence in his judgment and prudence. He was allowed by his comrades of the beach to be one of the smartest boatmen on the coast. My husband ascertained this, and he also agreed with me in my opinion of the fellow's respectability, and day after day I would enter the boat and my husband would stand watching me without the faintest misgiving of any sort in either of us.

On several occasions Hitchens carried me out to so great a distance that the features of the land were indistinguishable, and these long trips I enjoyed most of all; they were like voyages, and when I stepped on shore I would feel as though I had just arrived from the other side of the world.

We had now been a day over three weeks at Piertown. The weather had continued fine and warm throughout—in truth, a more beautiful October I never remember—and we had all benefited vastly by the change. But on the morning of this day my husband received a letter. He opened it, read it attentively, and exclaimed to me across the breakfast table, 'I shall have to leave you for a couple of days.'

'Why?' I asked.

He passed the letter to me: it was a business letter, addressed to him by his clerk. The nature of the business does not concern us; enough that the call was important and peremptory. The business, my husband said, would certainly detain him in Bath until the hour of the departure of a late train on the following night, if indeed he should be able to return then.

I packed his handbag, and Mary and I walked with him to the railway station. I kissed him, and we parted.

My sister and I returned home to take the children to the sands. We passed the morning under the cliffs, talking and reading and playing with the children. It was a bright day, but I afterwards remembered noticing that the blue of the heavens was wanting in the beautiful clear vividness of hue of the preceding days. The azure had a somewhat dim and soiled look, such as one might fancy it would exhibit in a very fine, thin dust-storm. I also afterwards remembered having observed that there was a certain brassiness in the glare of the sun, as if his light were the reflection of his own pure golden beams cast by a surface of burnished brass or copper. These things I afterwards recollected I had noticed, yet I do not remember that I spoke of them to my sister.

We dined at one o'clock. The road from our house to the sands carried us past the entrance to the pier. As we leisurely strolled, Bill Hitchens lifted his breast from the post which he was overhanging, and approached us with a respectful salutation of his hand to his brow.

'Will you be going out this afternoon, lady?' he asked.

'My husband has been called away,' I replied, 'and I do not feel as if I should care to go upon the water during his absence.'

'You will find the afternoon tedious, dear,' said Mary.

'It's a beautiful day, lady,' said the boatman. 'There's a nice little air o' wind stirring. Couldn't ask for a prettier day for a sail, lady.'

'It is somewhat cloudy,' said I, directing my gaze at the sky.

'Fine weather clouds, lady,' said the boatman. 'Keep your sight upon 'em for a bit and you'll find they're scarcely moving.'

'That is true,' said I.

'If you go,' said Mary, 'I will take Johnny and baby for a drive.'

'You'll soon be leaving Piertown, lady, worse luck!' said the boatman, with an insinuating grin. 'This here fine weather ain't a-going to last neither. It won't be long afore we'll be laying our boats up. It may be blowing hard to-morrow, lady, and it may keep on blowing until your time's up for retarning.'

I reflected and said, 'Well, Hitchens, you can get your boat ready for me by half-past two or a quarter to three. I'll be back by four,' said I, addressing Mary, as we walked home, 'and by that time you'll have returned. Do not keep baby out later than four,' and we talked of my husband and on home matters as we climbed the road that led to the level of the cliff.

At a quarter-past two I was ready to walk to the pier for a trip which I thought might likely enough prove my last, and which was not to exceed an hour and a quarter. I was dressed in the costume in which I usually made these excursions—in a blue serge dress, a warm jacket, and a sailor's hat of grey straw. An old-fashioned fly stood at the door waiting for Mary and the nurse and children. I took baby in my arms and kissed her, and I lifted Johnny and kissed him and saw the little party into the fly, which drove off.

I lingered a moment or two. A strange sense of loneliness suddenly possessed me. I cannot imagine what could have caused it if it were not the silence that followed upon the fly driving off, together with the thought that my husband was away. I entered the little parlour to ascertain the time by the clock on the mantelpiece, for my watch had stopped and I had left it in my bedroom. Upon the table lay a pair of baby's shoes, and a horse and cart that my husband had bought for Johnny was upon the floor. As I looked at these things I was again visited by an unaccountable feeling of loneliness. But it could possess no possible signification to me, and passing out of the house I closed the hall-door and walked briskly down to the pier.

The boat was ready. I entered her, and Hitchens rowed out of the harbour. The surface of the water was smooth, for the small breeze of the morning had weakened and was now no more than a draught of air; but the sea undulated with what sailors call 'a swell,' upon which the boat rose and sank with a sensation of cradling that was singularly soothing to me. The horizon was somewhat misty, and I observed that the extremities of the coast on either hand in the distance were blurred, showing indeed as though they were mirrored in a looking-glass upon which you had slightly breathed.

'It looks somewhat foggy out upon the sea,' said I.

'Nothen but heat, lady, nothen but heat. I like to see fog myself with the wind out at Nothe. When that happens with fine weather it sinifies that fine weather's a-going to last.'

The figures of a few boatmen idly lounged upon the esplanade. A man in a white apron, smoking a pipe, stood in the door of one of the public-houses, watching us as the boat receded. A coastguardsman, stick in hand, leaned over the edge of the pier, gazing down at the little cluster of boats which swayed upon the gently heaving water of the harbour. The sun shone upon some bright gilt sign of a cock, or bird of some sort, over the door of one of the public-houses; and next door to this sign was another, the painted head and bust of a woman eagerly inclining forwards, with the right arm advanced and a wreath in her hand. It had probably been the figure-head of a ship.

These little details of the picture I remember remarking as I looked at the shore whilst the boat leisurely drew away. What a dull, motionless place did Piertown seem! The main street climbing the hill was visible past the curve of the pier, and only two figures were to be seen ascending it.

'I cannot understand how you men get a living,' said I to Bill Hitchens.

'We don't onderstand it ourselves, lady,' said he.

'You are boatmen, but nobody hires your boats,' said I. 'How do you live?'

'It's a riddle, mum,' answered Hitchens, 'and there ain't no answer to it.'

'Yet those boatmen,' said I, 'who are standing upon the esplanade are comfortably dressed, they appear neat and clean, their clothes may be rough but they are fairly good and warm, they are all smoking and I suppose they have to pay for the tobacco they smoke; they, and others like them, are constantly in and out of the public-houses, and the beer which they drink must cost them money. How do they manage?'

'I've been man and boy getting on for eight and forty years upon that there beach,' said Bill Hitchens, 'and if you ask me to tell you how me and the likes of me manages, my answer is, lady, I gives it up.'

We were silent, and I continued to look at the shore and to admire the scene of it.

'The time was,' said Bill Hitchens meditatively, 'when I hoped to live to see the day as 'ud find me the landlord of a public-house. When all's said and done, lady, I don't know that a plain man like myself could ask for a more enjoyable berth than a public. Take a dark, wet, cold night, blowing hard and the air full of snow and hail. Only think of the pleasure of opening the door just to look out, so as to be able to step back again into the light and warmth and all the different smells of the liquors,' he added, snuffing. 'Only think how pleasingly the time flies in yarning with customers. Then, if ever ye stand in need of a drain, there it is—anything ye like and nothen to pay; 'cos when a landlord drinks it's always at the expense of his customers, whether they knows it or not. Then think again, lady, of a snug little parlour at the back, all shining with clean glasses and mugs like silver, with a warm fire and a kettle of boiling water always ready—ah!' He broke off with a deep sigh.

'I'll take an oar,' said I.

'Lor' bless me!' he cried, running his eyes over the boat. 'I've forgotten to ship a pair of sculls for you,' by which term he signified the light oars he was in the habit of placing in the boat for my use.

'The oar you are rowing with will be too heavy for me, I fear,' said I.

I dorn't think it will, mum,' he answered. 'Suppose ye try it. After you're tired of rowing we'll hoist the sail, for we shall find more wind stirring when we get out furder.'

He adjusted the oar and I seated myself at it and began to row. He sat in the bows of the boat near the tall mast and I upon a hinder seat near to that end of the boat which I had heard him call the 'stern sheets.' I did not find the oar so heavy as I had imagined. The boatman had placed it so as to fairly balance it and I continued to swing it without much trouble.

But after I had been rowing a few minutes the pressure of the handle of the oar in my grasp caused my rings to hurt me. I endured the inconvenience until it became a pain; then, tilting the oar and supporting it by my elbow, I pulled off my rings—that is to say, my wedding-ring and two others, all that I wore—and placed them by my side on the sail, which lay in a sort of bundle along the seats. I never had any superstitious feeling about my wedding-ring. Over and over again had I removed it to wash my hands. With many women, when once the wedding-ring is on, it is on for ever. Well would it have been for me had I possessed the sentiment of tender and graceful superstition that influences most wives in this way.

My rings being removed I applied myself again to the oar, and for about a quarter of an hour Bill Hitchens and I continued to row the boat out into the open sea. By this time we had reached a distance of a mile from the land. The faint air had been slowly freshening into a little breeze, and the water was rippling briskly against the side of the boat. I was now tired of rowing, and, asking Bill Hitchens to take the oar from me, I rose from my seat and sat down near the tiller.

'May as well hoist the sail now, lady, don't ye think?' said Bill Hitchens.

'Yes, you can hoist the sail,' said I, 'but I do not wish to go too far from the land. What o'clock is it?'

He extracted an old silver watch from somewhere under his jersey and gave me the time.

'I wish to be home by about a quarter past four,' said I.

He answered that he would see to it, and, seizing hold of a rope which passed through the top of the mast, he hoisted the sail. He then came to where I was sitting, and set the little sail upon the mast at the stern, and when this was done he grasped the tiller, and the boat, feeling the pressure of the breeze in her broad canvas—for though she was a small boat she carried a sail that I would think was disproportionately large for her size—heeled over and cut through the water on her side very quickly.

'It's a nice soldier's wind for the land, lady,' said the boatman.

'What is a soldier's wind?' I asked.

'Why,' he answered, 'a wind that allows ye to go there and back wherever ye may be bound to.'

'The coast looks a long way off, Hitchens.'

'It's vurking up a bit hazy, lady, but there's nothen to hurt.'

'I expect the sky will be overcast before sunset,' said I. 'Do you see that bank of clouds hazily peering through the air over the coast there?' and I indicated a portion of the land which certainly did not lie in the direction whence the wind was blowing; so that it was plain to me, ignorant as I was in all such matters, though my perception had been sharpened a little by being much upon the water, and by listening to Bill Hitchens discoursing upon the several aspects of his calling—I say it was plain to me that those clouds were working their way up over the land, and that if they did not promise a change of weather they must certainly betoken a shift of wind.

The boatman cast his eyes carelessly towards the coast and said 'that there was nothing to hurt in them clouds, that he rather believed they were settling away instead of rising,' and then he changed the subject by asking me if my husband had gone to London, and if I had ever seen London, and if it was as big a place as folks pretended it to be.

CHAPTER III
'WHO AM I?'

I SAT looking about me, now watching the pretty wreaths of foam spring past the sides of the boat, now gazing at the land whose features had blended into a long, dark, compact, but hazy line, sometimes addressing questions to Bill Hitchens, and always enjoying what to me was the exquisitely pleasurable sensation of the boat buoyantly sweeping over the little feathering ripples, when, my eyes going on a sudden to my left hand, I cried out, 'Oh, where are my rings?'

'Your rings, lady?' exclaimed the boatman.

'Yes, my rings. Did you not see me take off my rings? I put them on the sail that lay near me. Oh, where are they, where are they? I cannot lose them. One is my wedding-ring and the other two are my husband's gifts. Oh, Hitchens, where are they?' I cried, and, with a passion of eagerness and fear, I hunted over the bottom of the boat with my eyes, peering and straining my gaze at every crevice and hollow.

'Now be calm, lady,' said Hitchens, 'it'll come right. The rings can't be fur off. Let me question you. Where did you say you put 'em?'

'That sail up there lay along the seats, and I put my rings on it, on a corner of it that was close to me. I believed that they would be safe there. They could not slide off canvas.'

The man's face fell as he looked into the bottom of the boat.

'If you'll catch hold of this here tiller, lady,' said he, 'I'll have a search. They can't be fur off, I hope,' he added in a voice meant to encourage me.

I put my hand on the tiller, but hardly knew what more to do with it than to keep it steady. My distress was exquisite. When I looked over the bottom of the boat and could not see any glitter of my wedding-ring and the other two rings I shivered as though possessed with a passion of grief. Oh, if I had been careless in removing my rings, it shocked me to the heart to think of losing them—of losing my wedding-ring, that symbol of my wedded love and happiness.

'Do you see any signs of them?' I cried to Hitchens. 'I shall not mind the loss of the other rings, but I must have my wedding-ring—I must not lose it—I *cannot* lose my wedding-ring.'

The poor fellow, with a face of real concern, groped about the bottom of the boat. He lifted up a board, and carefully felt about with his hand in some water that lay in a kind of well. But I was sure that if the rings were not to be seen at once they would not be seen at all, because there were three of them, and one at least must certainly be visible: for though there were many crevices in the boat they were all very shallow, and the gleam of the rings would be instantly perceptible.

'I am afraid, lady,' exclaimed the boatman, standing up, 'that they've gone overboard.'

I moaned.

'I didn't,' he continued, 'take any notice of 'em, and in my sudden whipping up of the sail they must have been chucked ower the side. It's a bad job true-ly,' and again he bent his figure to look.

I now realised that I had lost my rings; it had not been a loss to be instantly felt and understood. My wedding-ring was gone; another wedding-ring I might easily buy, but the one that was consecrated to me by memory, the ring with which my husband had made me his wife, was irrecoverably gone, and as I looked upon my bare hand I wept, and then for a third time was I visited with a cold heart-subduing feeling of loneliness.

'Turn the boat for the land,' I said to Hitchens. 'I am miserable and want to get home.'

As he came to the tiller he directed a look out at the west, or rather I should say in the direction of the coast, for the haze had thickened magically within the last ten minutes or so, and though the land was scarcely above three miles distant it was little more than a dim shadow, that seemed to be fading out even as we looked. But I was still so grieved and distracted by the loss of my wedding-ring that I had no eyes save for my bare hand, and no thoughts save for what was at the bottom of the sea.

'The wind's shifted,' said Hitchens. 'It is off the land. You was right, lady, arter all. Them clouds *was* a-coming up. We shall have to ratch home.'

He dragged at some ropes which held the corners of the sails, and, moving his tiller, caused the boat to turn; but she did not turn so as to point the head for the land.

'Why do you not steer for Piertown?' I said.

'The wind's come dead foul, lady. We shall have to ratch home.'

'What do you mean by "ratch"?'

'We shall have to tack—we shall have to beat back.'

I did not understand his language, but neither would I tease him by questions. Now I was sensible that the wind had increased and was still increasing. I lifted up my eyes and judged that the wind was coming out of a great heap of cloud which lay over the land—the heap of cloud whose brows I had noticed rising above the edge of the cliff; but the mass had since then risen high, and there was a shadow upon it as if rain were falling. The boat lay sharply over upon her side, and her stem, as it tore through the water, made a strange stealthy noise of hissing as though it were red hot.

'The land is fading out of sight,' said I.

'Ay, it's drawed down thicker than I expected,' answered the boatman.

'Is not the wind very high?'

'It's blowing a nice sailing breeze,' he answered; 'though it's a pity it's shifted, as you're in a hurry to get home.'

But as he gazed round the sea I seemed to witness an expression of uneasiness in his face. It appeared to me that he was sailing away from the land. I was alarmed, and questioned him. He drew a piece of chalk from his pocket and first marked down upon the seat the situation of the coast, then the situation of the boat, and then the process of tacking, and how we should have to sail at angles in order to reach Piertown harbour.

'What time is it, Hitchens?'

He looked at his watch and said, 'Just upon the hour of four.'

'Oh! how the time has flown! Already four! When shall we arrive, do you think?'

'I'm afeared,' he answered, 'that I sha'n't be able to put ye ashore much before five.'

'But the atmosphere continues to grow thicker. Look! some parts of the coast are invisible. If you should lose sight of the coast, how will you be able to steer for it?'

'We'll find our way home all right, lady,' he exclaimed cheerfully. 'Don't be afeared. The loss of them there rings has worried ye, as well it might, and I'd give half the worth of this boat to be able to fish 'em up.'

I sat silent and motionless, gazing at the slowly dissolving line of coast over the gunwale. The water was now streaming in lines, and every line had its edging of spray, and often from these little foaming ridges there would flash a handful of glittering crystals, as though some hand within were hurling diamonds and prisms through the curling head of the brine. The thickness of the atmosphere lay around the sea, and so shrunk the plain of water that it looked no more than a lake in size. There was also the gloom of gathering clouds in the air, not only of the clouds which were rising off the land, but of vapour forming overhead and sailing athwart the course of the boat in dirty shreds and rags of the stuff that is called by sailors 'scud!'

'Will you hold the tiller for a moment, lady?' said the boatman. 'There's summat wrong with——' and he pronounced a technical word which I do not remember.

I grasped the tiller and he rose and went into the bows of the boat, where he paused for a moment, looking up; he then got upon the gunwale of the boat and stood with his back to the sea, with one hand upon a rope that ran from the front mast down to the bowsprit. He preserved that posture of standing and supporting himself and looking upwards whilst one might count ten; then let go of the rope, brought his hands together over his heart and, with a kind of short rattling groan, fell backwards.

The boat sat low on the water, and as the poor fellow therefore fell from no height, he rose to the surface before the boat had gone past him by her own length; he floated on his back, and made no effort to swim; I do not remember witnessing a single struggle in him; whence I judged, when I was able to think, that he had fallen dead from the gunwale of his little vessel; and the manner in which he had seemed to clutch at his heart, and the short rattling groan that he had delivered, confirmed me in this belief.

When he fell I sprang to my feet with a shriek of horror. For some moments, which would have been precious had he been alive and struggling, I did not know what to do. My heart stood still, I could not draw a breath. Then with lightning speed there swept into my head the thought that if he were drowned I should be alone, and, being alone, I should be absolutely helpless; and this thought electrified me, and not only enabled me to reflect, but gave me power to act. For, far more swiftly than I can relate what I did, yes, even though I was talking to you instead of writing, I grasped one of the long heavy oars and launched it towards the figure of the man as a spear is hurled. I needed, indeed, the strength of terror to accomplish this; at another time it would have taxed my strength to merely drag the oar to the side and let it fall.

The boat had been sailing fast when the poor man dropped from the gunwale, but when I sprang up I released the tiller, which I had been holding steady, having no knowledge whatever of steering, and the boat being released from the government of her helm, flew round into the wind, but not until she had left the body of the man a long distance behind; and then she stood upright upon the water, with her sails angrily shaking. Wild with thought and fear, wild with despair and terror, I kept my eyes fastened upon the body of the man. Oh, I cried to myself, can he not swim? Will he not attempt to reach the oar? And I screamed out his name, pointing to the direction where the oar lay. But as I continued to point and scream out his name the body sank. It vanished instantly, as though it had been desperately jerked under water by some hidden grasp or fang below. I stood straining my gaze, not knowing but that he might rise again, and then it was that the boat, being pointed a little away from the wind by the beat of the small, short waves, was smitten by the blast in her forward canvas; she turned and rushed through the water, whitening it, and lying dangerously down under the weight of her sails; but after she had started she, of her own accord, wound round into the wind again and sat upright, plunging quickly with her canvas rattling, and time after time this process was repeated, whilst I stood staring round me, seeing nothing of the land, beholding nothing, but the contracted plain of the ocean, around which the haze or fog stood as a wall, whilst overhead the sky was of the colour of slate, shadowed by speeding wings of scud.

It was raining, and when I looked in the direction whence the wind was blowing, the rain that drove aslant splashed in my face. I thought to myself, What will next happen? The boat will overset, and I shall be drowned! What am I to do?—what am I to do? And as I thought thus, weeping bitterly, and wringing my hands in the extremity of my grief and fright, the boat heeled over and depressed her side so low that the white foam she churned up flashed and roared to the level of the line of her gunwale. I grasped the opposite side to save myself from falling, by which I no doubt saved my life, because, had I slipped and staggered to the depressed side, my weight must certainly have capsized the boat. She rushed like an arrow round again into the wind and then stopped dead, plunging yet more sharply.

I wrung my hands again and cried aloud, What am I to do? But, happily, I had sense enough to understand that the very first thing to be done was to lower the sail, and as I had repeatedly observed poor Hitchens hoist the tall sheet of canvas, I knew what rope to undo, and, stepping over the seats, I released the rope, and, the boat being at that moment with her head pointing into the wind, the sail fell, but in falling it enveloped me and threw me down, and it was some minutes before I succeeded in extricating myself.

This, to be sure, was a trifling accident, for I was not in the least degree hurt, but the being thrown down and smothered by the canvas immeasurably heightened my distress and terror; I trembled from head to foot, my knees yielded under me, and I was forced to sit. It was raining hard, and the wet made the wind feel cruelly cold as it rushed athwart the boat, whipping the crests off the waves into an angry showering of spray. But after a little I began to find some faint comfort in the belief that the boat was stationary. Alas, how great was my ignorance! Because she did not appear to sail, and because she no longer lay dangerously over, I believed she was stationary. Yet two little sails were still set, a triangular sail at the bowsprit and a small square sail at the stern, and I must have been crazed indeed not to guess that whilst this canvas remained exposed the light fabric would be blown along by the wind, either sideways or forward, and that, as the wind blew directly from the west, every minute was widening my distance from Piertown.

But not understanding this, I found some heart in the belief that the boat was stationary, and I tried to comfort myself in other ways. I said to myself, this rain may be a passing shower, the weather will brighten presently, the boat will be in view from the coast, my situation will be guessed at by the boatmen who hang about the Esplanade, and they will put off to rescue me. And I also said to myself, even if this weather should not clear up, even if I remain out here invisible from the land, yet when my sister finds that it grows dark and I have not returned, she is sure to go down to the harbour and offer rewards for my rescue, and I may count upon several boats coming out to search for me.

Thus I thought, striving to give myself heart. But oh, the desolation of that mist-environed stretch of steel-grey water—chilly, leaping, and streaming in froth! Oh, the cruel cold of the rain-laden wind pouring shrilly past my ears and penetrating my wet clothes till my breast felt like marble! Not even now could I realise my situation. I knew that I was alone and that I was helpless, but the horizon of my fears and wretchedness was contained in these simple perceptions. I did not believe that I should perish. I was sure that succour would come, and my sufferings now lay in the agony of expectation, in the present and heart-breaking torment of waiting.

The time passed, the shadow of the evening entered the gloom of the afternoon. It continued to rain, and the horizon lay shrouded close to the boat, but I believe there was no increase in the wind: I noticed no increase. But indeed I was too ignorant, too despairful, too heartbroken to heed the weather, unless it were to observe, with eyes half-blind with my own tears and the flying rain that the sea was darkening, that the thickness lay close around the boat, and that nothing ever came out of that thickness save the dusky shapes of waves.

'Am I to be out in this boat all night?' I thought to myself. 'If so, I shall die of cold and exhaustion. I cannot pass the whole long night alone in this open boat in the rain, and in the bitter cold wind, wet through to the skin as I already am, without anybody to speak to, without food or drink, without a ray of light for my eyes to find comfort in resting on. O God! O God! I cried, and I went down upon my knees in the boat, and, clasping my hands, I gazed upwards into the grey, wet shadow of the sky, under which the naked mast of the boat was reeling, and I prayed to God to be with me, to watch over me, to bring help to me before I expired of fear and cold, and to return me to my sister, and to my little ones who were waiting for me.

And now I scarcely know how to proceed. What followed was a passage—a horribly long passage—of mental suffering incommunicable by the pen, nay scarcely to be remembered or understood by the sufferer herself. It fell dark, and the black night came, the blacker because there was no moon and because of the rain and the mist. I had gathered the wet cloths of the sail about me as a sort of shelter, and I sat with my head above the line of the gunwale, for ever looking to left and to right, and to right and to left, and never seeing more than the pale, near gleam of froth. At times thought grew maddening, and I shrieked like one in a fit or like a woman insane. It was not the fear of death that maddened me, it was not the anguish of the cold and the wet, nor even the fearful loneliness of my situation, a loneliness that cannot be imagined, for what magic is there in ink to figure the impenetrable blackness of the night, to imitate the snapping and sobbing sounds of the water and the hissing of the wind? No, it was the thought of my husband and my children; and it was chiefly the thought of my children. Again and again, when my mind went to them, I would catch myself moaning, and again and again I shrieked. With the eye of imagination I saw them sleeping: I saw my darling boy slumbering restfully in his little bed, I saw my baby asleep in her little cot; I bent over them in fancy; I kissed the golden hair of my boy, and I kissed the soft cheek of my baby; and then the yearnings of my heart grew into agony insupportable.

And there was a dreadful fancy that again and again visited me. Amid the crawling and blinking foam over the boat's side I sometimes imagined I saw the body of Hitchens. It came and went. I knew it was a deception of the senses, yet I stared as though it were there indeed. Sometimes there would come a sound in the wind that resembled the groan he had uttered when he fell overboard.

At some hour of the night, but whether before or after midnight I could not have told, I was looking over the right side of the boat when a large shadow burst out of the darkness close to. It swept by wrapped in gloom. It was a vessel, and she whitened the throbbing dusky surface over which she passed with a confused tumble of froth. There was not a single spot of light upon her. Her sails blended with the midnight obscurity, and were indistinguishable. Indeed she was to be heard rather than seen, for the noise of the wind was strong and shrill in her rigging, and the sound of her passage through the water was like a rending of satin. She was visible, and then she was gone even as I looked.

All night long it rained, and it was raining at daybreak in a fine thin drizzle. The sea was shrouded as on the previous afternoon. When the cold and iron grey of the dawn was upon the atmosphere, I feebly lifted up my head, marvelling to find myself alive. I looked about me with my eyes as languid as those of a dying person's, and beheld nothing but the streaming waters running out of the haze on one side and vanishing in the haze on the other side. Had I then possessed the knowledge of the sea that I afterwards gained, I might have known by the character of the waves that during the night the boat had been swept a long distance out. The billows were large and heavy, and the movements of the boat, whose sails were too small to steady her, were wild. Yet she rose and fell buoyantly. These things I afterwards recollected.

I was without hunger, but the presence of daylight sharpening my faculties somewhat I felt thirsty, and no sooner was I conscious of the sensation of thirst than the perception that it was not to be assuaged raised it into a torment. There was water in the bottom of the boat; I dipped my finger into one of the puddles and put the moisture to my lips. It was brackish, almost indeed as salt as the water of the sea. I pressed my parched lips to the sodden sail, which I had pulled over my shoulders, and the moisture of it was as salt as the puddle I had dipped my finger into.

And now, after this time, I have but a very indistinct recollection of what followed. All my memories are vague, as though I had dimly dreamed of what I saw and suffered. I recollect that I felt shockingly ill, and that I believed I was dying. I recollect that during some hour of this day I beheld a smudge in the grey shadow of mist and rain on my right, that it kindled an instant's hope in me, that I held open with difficulty my heavy wet eyelids and watched it in a sickly and fainting way, believing it might prove a boat sent in search of me. I followed it with my gaze until it melted away in the thickness. I recollect that the day passed, and that the blackness of a second night came; but, this remembered, all else is a blank in my brain.

I opened my eyes and found myself in gloom. A few inches above me was a shelf; I supposed it to be a shelf. Dim as the light was, there was enough of it to enable me to see that what was stretched just above me was not part of a ceiling. I lay looking at it. I then turned my head on to my right cheek and beheld a wall. I touched it to make sure. I passed my hand slowly over it, and then looked up again at the shelf that was stretched over my head. I then turned my head and perceived a little circle of greenish light. I stared at this strange glimmering disk of light for a long while, again looked upwards, and again feebly passed my hand over the wall.

I did not ask myself where I was; I felt no curiosity. I was as one in whom an intellect has been suddenly created, and who passively accepts what the sight rests on. I lay turning my head from cheek to cheek for some ten minutes or a quarter of an hour, during which my eyes, having grown used to the gloom that was faintly touched by that circle of greenish light, began to distinguish objects. And first I saw that I was in a very little dark room, lying upon a sort of shelf which, with the upper shelf, resembled a long box, of which one side was wanting; and scarcely had I perceived that I was in a little dark room than I became sensible that I was upon the water: for, as I lay on the shelf, I felt that my body was rolled from side to side, and I also felt an upwards motion and then a downwards motion, and I knew that I was at sea.

Then I thought to myself, I am in the cabin of a ship. But how did I get here and who am I? Having said to myself *Who am I?* I repeated the words over and over again; but as yet without surprise, without terror. The question haunted my mind with languid iteration, but it induced no emotion. I felt sick and extraordinarily weak. Something irritated my brow, and, lifting my hand, I found my right temple and the eyebrow and a portion of the nose as far as the bridge of it pasted over with some hard substance. I ran my fingers over this substance, but without wonderment, and then my arm fell exhausted to my side, and feebly turning my head on to my left cheek, I stared at the glimmering green disc, whilst I kept on thinking to myself, but without agitation or fear, *Who am I?*

It did not strike me as in the least degree strange that I should not know who I was. I lay looking, and I saw a man's coat swinging by a nail near the little circle of dim light. I also saw a common cane-bottom chair and a dark chest, which I have since learnt to call by its proper name of 'locker.' From the ceiling of this little room there swung, suspended by thin brass chains, a strange-looking lamp, formed of a globe of metal with a glass chimney. I continued to watch that lamp swing until my eyelids closed, but whether I fainted or slumbered I am unable to say.

When I awoke or regained consciousness the glimmering circle of glass had changed from dim green into bright yellow. It rippled with brilliance as from the reflection of sunshine upon water, and there was daylight in the little cabin. I heard the sound of a fiddle and the voice of a man singing. The sounds were on the other side of the wall which I had felt over with my hand when I first awoke. Presently the music ceased, and almost at the moment that it ceased I heard the rattle of a door-handle and what looked to be a shapeless bulk stood at my side.

On straining my dim sight I saw that the figure was that of an immensely fat man. He stood with his back to the circular window, and for some while I was unable to discern his features. Meanwhile he stared at me as though there was nothing in my fixed look to satisfy him that I was alive or dead. His face was perfectly round and his cheeks puffed out as if he were in the act of blowing. Upon his upper lip were a few short straggling hairs, iron grey; his hair was scanty and grizzled; his complexion was a brick red, apparently from exposure to weather. Yet his fat face was deprived of the expression of stupid good nature that one commonly finds in such countenances by a pair of heavy, shaggy, almost white eyebrows, which, coming close together over the top of his nose, stamped the look of an habitual frown upon his forehead. His eyes were small, black and piercing, and his age might have been anything between fifty and sixty. He wore a red cap, the tasselled point of which fell over his ear, and his dress consisted of a soiled and well-worn pilot-coat hanging loose over an equally soiled and well-worn velveteen jacket. A large shawl was wound round his neck, and there were gold hoops in his ears. These points I afterwards witnessed. All that

I now observed was his large round face of a dusky crimson and the small black eyes in it fixed upon me.

At last he exclaimed, in a deep voice: 'Tiens, vous voilà enfin éveillée, après trois jours de sommeil! Eh bien, j'espère que maintenant vous soyez en état de prendre quelque nourriture et de me dire ce que vous êtes. Peste! que n'avez-vous donc échappé! C'est vrai les femmes peuvent supporter plus que les hommes. Elles ne sont pas si facilement écrasées que nous autres pauvres diables.'

I listened to these words and understood them, but I did not know they were French. Yet though I could not have given a name to the tongue in which the man spoke I knew what he said. My knowledge of French suffered me to read it and slightly understand it when spoken, but I was unable to converse in it.

What he had said was: 'So then you are awake at last! Three days of sleep! Well, now you will be able to eat and drink, I hope, and tell me who you are. Peste! what an escape! But women have more endurance than men. They are not so easily destroyed as us poor devils.'

I gazed at him without answering. He addressed me again in French.

'What do you say?' I whispered.

'Aha! you are Angleesh,' exclaimed the man in his deep voice, and he added in French, 'Stop! I will go and fetch Alphonse.'

His shapeless bulk moved away from the side of the shelf and I lay motionless, with my eyes fixed upon the bright circle of glass upon which the reflection of sunny waters without was dancing. But I do not know what I thought of. I cannot remember that any sort of determinable idea visited me. My mind seemed empty, with one strange question for ever dully echoing in it: *Who am I?* Yet I also seemed to know that I was not mad. I could not tell who I was, but I felt that I was not mad. I do not say that my instincts assured me of this; I seemed to be sensible of it passively. It was a perception independent of all effort of mind, a knowledge wholly involuntary as the action of the heart is involuntary.

In a few minutes I heard the door-handle rattle again and two figures came to the side of the shelf on which I lay. One was the same stout personage that had previously visited me; the other was a clean, fresh-looking young man of the age of four or five and twenty, smoothly shaven, with coal black hair and eyes, his face of a pronounced French type. He was fairly well dressed in a suit of grey, and his white shirt collar was buttoned low so as to expose the whole of his long throat and even a portion of his chest. His posture suggested an air of habitual attention and respect, and after he had peered a while and observed that my eyes were open he removed his cap.

'Speak to her Alphonse,' said the large stout man.

'How do you do, madame? How do you now feel?' said the younger man in good English, pronouncing the words with an excellent accent.

I answered faintly, 'I believe I am dying. Where am I?'

'Oh,' he exclaimed quickly, 'you have not eaten, you have not drunken. It is impossible for people to live unless they eat and drink.'

He then addressed himself hurriedly to the fat man, who acquiesced with a grunt and a gesture of the hand. The young man went out, whilst the other remained at my side, fixedly staring at me. Even had I been able to exert my mind for conversation I could not have found my voice. It pained me to whisper. The stout man addressed me once in barbarous English; I languidly gazed at him in silence through my half-closed eyelids, and no more was said until the young man returned, bearing in one hand a cup and saucer and in the other hand a tumbler. The cup contained some warm soup; the tumbler some weak brandy and water. Now ensued a brief discussion between the two men as to whether the brandy should be administered before the soup or the soup before the brandy. The younger man's views prevailed and, correctly judging that I was unable to feed myself, he drew the cane-bottom chair to my side, seated himself and fed me.

The fat man stood with a stolid countenance, looking on. When I had swallowed the soup the young man applied the tumbler to my lips and I slowly drank.

'Now,' said the young man, 'do you feel more comfortable?'

I whispered that I felt better.

'That is right,' said he. 'You must keep quiet whether you sleep or not. I am not a doctor, but I know a thing or two. I will visit you again in two hours with more soup and *eau-de-vie*.' And he said to the fat man in his native tongue, 'Come, uncle, she will do. She will not die. Let us leave her.'

They then withdrew.

CHAPTER IV
ALPHONSE'S CONJECTURES

I TURNED my face to the wall and closed my eyes, and two hours, and perhaps more than two hours, passed, during which I did not sleep. I then opened my eyes and looked about me. I had intelligence enough to observe that my skirt and bodice had been removed and that I was wrapped in coarse, thick blankets. Then, feeling a kind of pricking pain about the forehead, I raised my hand to my brow and stroked with my finger-nails the strips of parchment-like stuff with which it was plaistered. What can this be? I thought; and then a most awful and terrible feeling of bewilderment possessed me. 'Who am I?' I cried in a voice that was still no louder than a whisper, 'and where am I? And—and—and——'

The young man whom the stout person had called Alphonse entered, bearing a bowl of soup and a glass of weak brandy and water upon a tray.

'Have you slept?' said he. I feebly shook my head. 'Well,' he exclaimed with the characteristic drawl of the Frenchman when he speaks English, 'it is not to be expected that you should sleep or that you should require sleep. You have been asleep for three days, and now you shall drink this soup and afterwards this cognac,' and, seating himself, he fed me and gave me to drink as before. He placed the tray upon the deck of the little cabin, and sat contemplating me for a while with an air of respect that seemed a habit in him, mingled with an expression of commiseration.

'You will get on,' he said, 'you will recover. You will be strong by the time we get to Toulon.'

'Toulon?' I said, speaking faintly.

'Yes, madame, Toulon. We are going to Toulon. This brick is now proceeding to that port.'

'Toulon?' I exclaimed.

'Madame knows without doubt where Toulon is?'

I gazed at him in silence.

'Does it fatigue you to speak?' said the young man whom I will hereafter call Alphonse, for by no other name did I ever know him.

'No,' said I in a whisper.

'Then tell me, madame, how it happened that you were in the miserable condition from which we rescued you?'

I tried to think, but I could not think. I forced my gaze inwards, but beheld nothing but blackness. I strained the vision of my mind, but it was like straining the balls of the sight at a dark wall in a midnight of blackness.

'You do not remember,' said the young Frenchman, shaking his head, 'the circumstances that brought you into the miserable condition from which we released you?'

'I can remember nothing,' I whispered. 'What was my condition?'

'Stop till you hear me tell you the story,' cried Alphonse, holding up two fingers, 'and then you will remember it all. This ship is what is called a brick [brig], and her name is *Notre Dame de Boulogne*. She belongs to the port of Boulogne-sur-Mer. Her owner and captain is Pierre Regnier. He is my uncle. He is the gentleman that was here with me. I, madame, by occupation am a waiter. I am a waiter at the Hôtel des Bains, Boulogne-sur-Mer. Our customers are nearly all English, and we *garçons* are expected to speak English. My native town is Toulon. My uncle Regnier, hearing that I had a holiday, says, "Come with me, Alphonse, in my brick to Toulon. That is my first port of destination." I consented, and that, madame, explains how it is that I am here. Well, it was three mornings ago—only think! It was a dark morning, and the hour was between five and six. It was foggy, and there was a little rain. One of the sailors saw a boat; it was close to us; before he could give the alarm we had struck it—slightly only, very luckily, or, madame, where would you now be? Our ropes tore down the boat's mast, and our sailors looking cried out that there was somebody in the boat. In some way the boat was entangled, and she was drawn along at our side, but the brick was sailing very slowly and the sea was not rough. My uncle Regnier commands the sailors to get into the boat, and they find you lying there. They bring you on board, and by this time there is a little daylight, and we see that there is blood upon your face, and that you are hurt here and here,' and Alphonse, as he spoke, pointed to his brow and to his nose, above the bridge of it. 'No sooner have we taken you on board than the boat liberates herself; she breaks away, and my uncle says, "Let her go." Well, we carry you into the cabin, and I put a mirror to your mouth and find that you breathe. I am not a doctor, but I know a thing or two. I ask my uncle for sticking-plaister, and first I wash the wounds and then I strap them up, and they cease to bleed. No doubt, madame, you were wounded by the boat's mast falling upon you. You reclined insensible in the boat when the mast fell. Was it so? Or was it the blow of the mast that made you insensible? No, naturally you would not remember. But it was certainly the mast that produced these wounds, for you lay with the mast upon you, and the sailors said they saw blood upon the mast. Luckily for you, madame, the side of the boat prevented all the weight of the mast from hitting you, or——' he shrugged his shoulders with a grimace and extended his hands. 'That now is all I can tell you.'

'You found me in a boat?' I said.

'Oh yes, madame; certainly, yes.'

'In a boat? Why was I in a boat? I cannot remember. Oh, what has happened to me? I have no memory! It has all gone! Where am I? What is this that has come to me?'

I raised myself upon my elbow, and instantly fell back, weak, sick, with an overwhelming feeling of horror upon me.

'Be calm, madame, be calm. I am not a doctor, but I know a thing or two. What is the memory? Tut! It will return. Chut! Before you arrive at Toulon you will have your memory. Let me hear your name, madame?'

'My name?' I exclaimed, and I thought and thought, and my mind seemed to wrestle and struggle within me, like something living that has been buried alive.

A light effort to recollect speedily grows into a sort of pain. This is true of trifles—as, for instance, a name, the recollection of which is not important, but you desire to pronounce it; the mind explores the gallery of the memory in vain for it, and the failure to find it grows into a worry and presently into a torment. Think, then, how it was with me when this young Frenchman asked me for my name, and I could not recall it! Recall it! Oh, that is to speak too mildly. Why, when I turned my mental gaze inwards it was like looking into a black abysm of a profundity impenetrable, upon the unreachable bottom of which was strown the wreckage of my past, were scattered the memorials of my life, for ever to be hidden from me, as I then believed.

'Let me hear your name, madame?' said the young Frenchman.

I thought and thought and answered, 'I cannot remember my name.'

'Not remember your name! But that is droll. Does it begin with A? Does it begin with B?' and he ran through the alphabet.

I listened, and all these letters sounded as idly upon my ear as the noise of the wind or the sound of passing waters.

'But you are English?' said he.

Again I thought and thought, and replied in a whisper, 'I cannot tell.'

He ejaculated in French. 'Will you not ask me some questions?' said he. 'Perhaps whilst you ask questions you will be able to recollect.'

'What shall I ask?' I answered, 'I remember nothing to ask.'

'Ask about the boat we found you in.'

'Yes, tell me about that boat,' said I.

'Aha!' cried he, 'you remember then. You know there was a boat?'

'I remember that you have told me that you took me from a boat.'

'Bravo! What does that signify? I am not a doctor, but I know a thing or two. Madame, if you can recollect what I say, memory you must have. Is it not so? The faculty you have. It is like a snake: all its body is asleep to the tip of its tail, but it is awake with its eyes. What do you think of that illustration, madame?'

I listened to him and viewed him in silence. I felt terribly weak and ill, but far worse to support than this feeling of weakness and illness was the horror that was upon me—a horror I could not understand, an inward presence that was made the more dreadful by my not being able to find a reason for it.

'Do you ask me about the boat?' said Alphonse. 'She had two masts, but one was broken by us. Beyond that——' he shrugged his shoulders. 'She slipped away when it was still dark. That was a pity. There would no doubt have been a name upon her.'

He ceased, and I observed that he fastened his eyes upon my hands. Then, after looking for some little time with attention at my face, he struck his forehead and cried, 'What a fool am I not earlier to have thought of it! An instant, madame. I will go and bring you your memory.'

He departed, and in a few minutes returned, holding a large oval handglass. 'Now,' he exclaimed, smiling, 'look at yourself, madame, and, though I am not a doctor, I pronounce that all will return to you.'

He elevated the glass and I looked at myself. But what did I see? Oh, reader, turn back to the description, in the opening pages of this story, of the lady seated at the head of the tea-table in the parlour of the house past the avenue of chestnuts; turn to it, and compare that face with what I saw reflected in the mirror held before me by the young Frenchman. The hair was snow-white; one eyebrow was snow-white; but the other eyebrow was concealed by a wide strip of white sticking-plaister. There were several such strips, which intersected each other upon the right brow, and one of them extended to the bridge of the nose, entirely sheathing the bone or cartilage, and leaving but little more than the extremity of the nose and the nostrils visible. The dark eyes were sunk and dim. The cheeks were hollow, and the complexion a dingy sallow, and as much of the brow as was left exposed and parts of the flesh of the face were covered with thin lines, as though traced by the point of a needle.

This was the face that looked out upon me from that hand-mirror. I stared at it, but I did not know it. Yet it did not terrify me, because I was unable to remember my former face, and therefore no shock of discovery attended my inspection. No, the sight of that dreadful face, with its milk-white hair and plaistered brow, with here and there a stain of dry blood upon the plaister, did not terrify me. I gazed as though beholding something that was not myself, and still I knew that the face that confronted me was my own face, and *this* it was, and not the face that deepened the indeterminable feeling of horror by quickening within me the awful silent question, '*Who am I?*'

'Now, madame,' exclaimed Alphonse, 'look steadily, and you will be able to pronounce your name and to remember.'

I closed my eyes, and when I opened them again he had removed the glass. I tried to speak, but though he inclined his head he seemed unable to hear me. On this he put his finger to his lips, and, after viewing me a while with an expression of pity and astonishment, he went softly out.

During the greater portion of the day my condition was one of stupor. Yet there were intervals when my mind was somewhat active. In these intervals I questioned myself, and I became acutely sensible of the indescribable feeling of horror that was upon me, and at such times I beheld, painted upon the gloom of the shelf on which I lay, the strange face that had gazed at me out of the hand-glass, and again and again I saw that head of a woman whose snow-white hair lay in long thick tresses about her shoulders and upon the rude bolster, though a portion of it was looped up and fastened in coils on the top of the head by hairpins, whose dark eyes were weak and without light, whose cheeks were hollow, and the skin of them and of her brow finely lined with innumerable wrinkles, whilst the whole countenance was rendered wild and repulsive by the lengths of white sticking-plaister that striped her temple.

Thrice during that day I was visited by the young Frenchman, who, on each occasion, brought me soup and some red wine. He was accompanied on his third visit by the great fat man, his uncle, and by a short man with an immense moustache and several days' growth of beard—a fierce-looking man, with dark knitted eyebrows, and gleaming black eyes with the savage stare of a gipsy in their intent regard. He was swathed in a coarse coat of pilot cloth, the skirts of which descended to his heels, and on his head was a fur cap which he did not remove as he stood viewing me.

They watched Alphonse feed me; I was scarcely conscious of their presence, and even if I heeded them, which I doubt, their inspection caused me no uneasiness, so languid were my faculties, so sick even unto death did I feel, so profoundly bewildered was I by the questions I asked myself, and by the blackness which lay upon the face of my mind when I turned my gaze inwards and searched it.

The fat man, Regnier, addressed Alphonse, who nodded and said to me: 'Well, madame, have you yet thought of your name?'

I answered, 'No.'

'And you cannot positively tell me that you are English?'

'I am speaking English; I speak no other tongue; I am English, then.'

'No,' he exclaimed, smiling, 'you might be American. And you say you do not speak any other language than English? How can you tell? You may have forgotten other languages in which you could converse. For example: you might be a German who speaks English excellently; and now by some caprice of the intellect you forget your German, and express yourself in English. I am not a doctor,' he added, wagging his head, 'but I know a thing or two.'

And, turning to the others, he addressed them swiftly and with great energy.

At some hour of the night I fell asleep. When I awoke, the sunshine was streaming brilliantly upon the little circular porthole. I lifted up my head and then raised myself upon my elbows and found myself stronger. I also felt better; the feeling that had been like approaching death was gone and the sickness was passed. I heard the sounds of a fiddle and of a man's voice singing in the next cabin. I listened to the voice and knew it to be that of the young Frenchman, Alphonse. The motion of the vessel was comparatively quiet. She was sailing somewhat on her side, but she rolled very lightly and the upwards and downwards movement was trifling. I felt that I had strength enough to sit up, but the upper shelf was too close to my head to suffer me to do so. I lay still and tried to think, and my thoughts ran thus:

Who am I? The face that I saw in the mirror yesterday is mine, but it begets no recollection. I do not recognise it. It is mine, yet it is a face that I have never before seen. How, then, can it be mine? But since that unknown face must be mine, who am I? I was found lying insensible and wounded—and here I laid my fingers upon the sticking-plaister upon my brow—in an open boat. She had two masts and that is all they can tell me.

How was it that I was in that boat? When did I enter her? I have been in this ship four days. How long was I in the boat, and from what part do I come? And then there was such a struggle of my mind that drops of perspiration started from my brow. I cannot express the agony that inward conflict caused me. I said to myself, Am I mad that I do not know who I am? What has happened to kill in me the power to recollect? What has happened to extinguish the vision in the eyes of my mind? All is black! I remember nothing down to the hour of my waking in this cabin; but since then everything that has happened, everything that has been said I remember. I can repeat the conversation of Alphonse, I can describe the appearance of his uncle and of the man who accompanied him; yes, and I can also describe accurately the face that I yesterday viewed in the glass which the young Frenchman held up before me. Therefore memory is not dead, neither can I be mad to be able to reason thus. Why then will not memory pronounce my name and give me back my past that I may know who I am, that I may know to what place to return? And I covered my face with my hands and wept.

Presently my tears ceased to flow. The strains of the fiddle and the voice of the singer were silent in the adjacent cabin. What is there to assist me to recover my memory? I thought; and I turned my eyes upon my figure as I lay stretched upon that sleeping-shelf, and looked at my ringless hands; and then my gaze ran with wildness over as much as I could see of the little cabin, but no suggestion came. My mind seemed torpid, unable of itself to receive or to produce ideas.

Somewhat later I heard a knock on the door. I exclaimed 'Come in!' and found that I had my voice again; yet there was nothing in the tone of it to help my memory. Alphonse entered and bade me good-morning.

'You look better, madame,' said he; 'do you feel better?'

'Yes; I feel stronger and better this morning.'

'Now, what did I tell you? Perhaps to-morrow you will be able to get up. Are you hungry?'

'I believe I can eat,' I said.

He snapped his fingers and instantly went out. When he returned he brought with him a cup of chocolate, some biscuits, marmalade and butter, and a boiled egg.

'What think you of this breakfast, madame, for a little brick? We have six hens on board, and this is the only egg this morning. Can you eat without help or shall I feed you?'

'I think I can eat without help if I sit up.'

On this he put his hand into the shelf over my head and took several boards out of it. I could now sit up; he placed the tray on my knees and I ate and drank.

'You are very good, you are very kind to me,' said I. 'What return shall I be able to make—what acknowledgment——' and I ceased eating to press my hand to my brow.

'Continue your breakfast,' said he. 'We will not talk of acknowledgment here. At Toulon you will obtain excellent medical advice. And now shall I tell you something?' added he, with a smile.

I looked at him.

'You are a lady. Your accent is that of the English lady of birth. I cannot mistake. I have waited upon many English ladies, and can always tell a lady of title. Do I assist your memory when I say that you are a lady of title?' Seeing that I shook my head, he continued: 'I call you madame. Perhaps I should say milady, or perhaps I should say miss. I beg your pardon, but you have no rings. A lady like you will have rings. Are they in the pocket of your dress? I ask, because if you saw your rings you might remember.'

'Where is my dress?'

'It is here,' and he stepped to a part of the cabin near the door and held up the dress.

I fastened my eyes upon it, but it suggested nothing.

'Has it a pocket?' I said.

He felt, and answered, 'Yes, and there is something in it,' and slipping in his hand he brought out a pocket handkerchief and a purse. 'Aha!' he cried. He examined the handkerchief and said: 'Here are two letters—"A. C." Pronounce them.' I did so. 'Now what do they signify?'

I turned them over and over and over again in my mind. 'They suggest nothing,' I said.

'Patience!' he exclaimed, and opening the purse he looked into it. 'Nothing but money,' he said, after examining the two or three divisions. 'Here is one pound; and here,' he continued, turning the money into his hand, 'are two half-crowns, sixpence, and some pennies. Is there nothing more?' He looked again, and exclaimed with a stamp of his foot: 'Nothing but money!'

CHAPTER V
ON BOARD 'NOTRE DAME'

ON the afternoon of this second day of my rescue, I found myself sufficiently strong to rise and repose in an old stuffed arm-chair, which the young Frenchman brought from an adjoining cabin. My limbs were weak and I trembled exceedingly. Nevertheless, I contrived to put on my dress, which had been thoroughly dried, so Alphonse told me, at the fire in the fore-part of the ship where the sailors' food was cooked.

This obliging and most humane young Frenchman also supplied me with certain toilet requisites of a homely kind indeed; yet the refreshment of washing my face and hands and of brushing my hair seemed to give me new life. The young Frenchman hung his oval hand-glass upon the cabin wall, and when he was gone I surveyed myself.

For a long while I could not lift the brush to my hair. I could only gaze and dumbly wonder with memory writhing sightless within me. I took the glass to the circular window; there was a strong yellow glow in the air outside, and the afternoon light focussed by that circular, tube-like window, lay upon my face. I intently examined my countenance, but I witnessed nothing that gave me the least hint of the past. I beheld a great quantity of snow-white hair, languid and lustreless dark eyes, the lids of which were half closed, hollow cheeks, a skin scored with innumerable fine lines, and the whole rendered repulsive by the stripes of stained plaister. When presently, having washed my face and hands, I began to brush my hair, many hairs came out on the brush. I passed my fingers through my tresses, and my hand came away with a quantity of white hair in it. I sighed and wondered, and trembled with weakness, and with the miserable horror that again visited me.

But now, instead of wearily thinking over and over again *'Who am I?'* my mind was haunted by those two letters 'A. C.,' which the young Frenchman had found in the corner of my handkerchief. I uttered them over and over again, fancying that the initials might suddenly expand into the full name, for I believed that if I could remember my name I should be able to recollect everything else.

When I had brushed and dressed my hair I drew forth my purse, and held it in my hand with my gaze riveted to it. But the black conflict in my mind grew too violent for my strength. I put the purse into my pocket and rocked myself in my chair, crying and crying until you would have thought my heart must break.

The Frenchman punctually brought me food and drink. He repeated that he was certain I was a lady of title; he had waited on too many female members of the British aristocracy to mistake. 'You will see that I am right, madame,' said he, and with this conviction his politeness increased, though more respectful his manner could not be.

During the evening I was visited by the uncle, whose speeches the young man translated.

'You are better,' exclaimed this large, fat, stolid man, who could not speak without nodding. 'Take the word of Captain Regnier, who is not often mistaken in his opinion. You are better, and you will soon be well. But you must recover your memory before we arrive at Toulon, that the British Consul at that port may be in a position to forward you to your friends.'

'But if I cannot remember, what is to become of me?' said I.

'Oh,' he answered, 'that will be the affair of the British Consul. Why should not a Consul earn his salary? These gentlemen have very easy times.'

'It is settled,' said Alphonse, 'that you are English. It will be the British Consul's business to find out all about you.'

'But if I cannot remember?'

'It will still be his business,' said Captain Regnier, who understood me, 'to find out all about you. My nephew is right. You are undoubtedly an English lady of distinction,' and he bowed to me with a strange motion of his bulky form.

The conversation continued in this strain for some time. They then left me.

The next afternoon the young Frenchman persuaded me to leave my cabin for the living room in which Captain Regnier, his nephew, and the mate Hénin took their meals. The young man gave me his arm and conducted me to the living room with the grace and tender attention of a perfectly well-bred gentleman. I found myself in a cabin many times larger than the tiny berth I had quitted, yet it was a very small apartment nevertheless. It is necessary that I should describe this interior that you may be able to understand what befel me later on. Figure a small square room, the ceiling within easy reach of the hand, the walls of a grimy colour that might have been either brown or yellow. In the centre of the ceiling was a large window, or rather several windows in a frame not unlike those glass frames in which cucumbers are grown. This window, as I afterwards came to know, would be called a skylight. There was a square opening in the deck a little distance behind this skylight, with a short steep flight of steps ascending to it. This opening would be called the hatch, and the deck was gained by passing through it. Close behind this ladder or flight of steps were the doors of two berths, one of which I occupied, and under the steps I observed a large cask, one end of which came very close to the door of my berth. Do not suppose that I immediately noticed these details. When I first entered that grimy and somewhat gloomy living room I took heed of little indeed. There was a small square table in the middle of the cabin and on either hand were rough dark fixed boxes termed lockers. A lamp of a curious pattern swung under a beam overhead. Such was the cabin of the brig *Notre Dame de Boulogne*.

Alphonse brought the arm-chair from my cabin and placed it near the table. He then placed a bundle of old numbers of the *Charivari* on my lap, and I turned the pages with a mechanical hand, incessantly saying to myself, 'What can the letters "A. C." stand for?'

I might know that it was a very fine evening by the clear crimson light that tinctured the glass in the frame overhead. The motion of the brig was easy and the lamp under the ceiling or upper-deck swung softly and regularly. I heard the murmur of hissing waters, and occasionally the voice of a man calling out abruptly echoed through the little opening that conducted to the deck.

I sat alone for some time. After I had been sitting alone for about half an hour, viewing the French comic paper with an eye that beheld nothing, since it was for ever inwards turned, Alphonse came out of the cabin next to mine with a fiddle in his hand.

'Now madame,' said he tapping it with the bow, 'tell me what this is.'

'It is a fiddle,' said I.

'Is not this a proof of memory?' cried he. 'How could you call it a fiddle if you did not know it to be a fiddle? and in this case to know is to remember.'

'You reason well,' I said smiling, and a sad smile I fear it was that I gave him. 'You converse as one who has been well educated.'

'I was very well educated, madame,' he answered. 'Those of our condition in England are not so well educated as we of France. We owe much to the priests. There are no such schoolmasters in the world. Otherwise I do not love priests. I am an infidel, and my opinions coincide with those of Voltaire and Volney. What is your religion, madame?'

I was unable to answer him. He put his fiddle against his shoulder and asked if he should play me a tune and sing me a song. I begged him to do so and forthwith he played and sang. He sang some merry French rhymes and the air was very lively and pretty.

Hardly had he ended his song when a lad with a dirty face and a quantity of brown hair hanging over his eyes came shambling down the stairs, bearing a large teapot and a dish of fried ham. Alphonse surveyed him with disgust, and withdrew to his cabin to put away his fiddle. The boy prepared the table for a repast that I afterwards understood was called supper by the Frenchmen. He lifted the lid of one of the large dark fixed boxes and brought out some plates and cups and saucers which he placed upon the table. He breathed hard and idled in his business of furnishing the table that he might stare at me. The meal, when ready, consisted of tea, ham, large brown biscuits, marmalade, and a great piece of cold sausage. Alphonse returned and stood looking at the table.

'This would not do for an English milord to sit down to,' said he, 'it would make him swear, and certainly your English milord knows how to swear. I should not like to wait upon company at such a table as this. But it is the sea—that sea which the English people love, but about which they know less than the French, though they talk much of their dominion maritime. Is there nothing on the table,' he added with a comprehensive gesture of the hand, 'that gives you an idea, madame?'

'Nothing.'

'Can you pronounce the names of what you see?'

'Yes.'

'How droll! how incredible! *Mon Dieu*, what a thing is the human intelligence! Because one little nerve or cell in the brain perhaps is wrong,' here he tapped his forehead, 'all is gloom. It is like turning off the gas. You go into a corner downstairs, you move a key no longer than that, and a great hotel of seventy bedrooms and thirty sitting-rooms is instantly plunged in darkness.'

He was interrupted by the arrival of his uncle, who, pulling off his red cap, gave me a bow and seated himself. I drank a cup of the tea; there was no milk, yet I found the beverage refreshing. I also ate some biscuit and marmalade. The conversation was all about myself. Captain Regnier's speeches were translated by Alphonse, and my mind was stimulated by what was said. I found myself capable of asking questions; but few were the questions I could find to ask. I had nothing to base them upon save the story of my rescue from an open boat, as it had been related to me, and the Frenchman had nothing more to tell me than that she was a boat with two masts.

'Was I alone in her?' I asked.

'Oh yes, you were alone,' answered Alphonse.

'How is it possible that I should be alone in an open boat?' I exclaimed.

'It was a pleasure-boat,' said Captain Regnier; 'without doubt you sailed on an excursion from some port, and were blown away to sea.'

'But alone!' I cried.

'You were alone, madame,' said Alphonse, and, eagerly addressing his uncle as though a fine idea had occurred to him, he exclaimed; 'Could you not tell by the build of the boat what her nationality was?'

Captain Regnier shrugged his shoulders until his ears were hidden. 'What is there of nationality in a boat of that size?' he answered. 'The boats of France, of England, of Europe in general—are they not very much alike—especially in the dark?'

'How long will it take you to arrive at Toulon?' I asked.

Again Captain Regnier, when this inquiry was translated, shrugged his shoulders and answered that it was a question for the wind.

'I will fetch the chart,' said Alphonse, 'and madame shall remark our situation for herself.'

He arose and walked to the forward part of the living room. I had supposed that that part was wholly walled off from the other portion of the ship. But the young Frenchman, putting his hand upon a ring in the middle of the wooden wall, drew open a sliding door. Captain Regnier said in broken English: 'My cabin is there.'

In a few minutes Alphonse returned with a large map or chart, which he unrolled upon a part of the table that he cleared to receive it. It was too dark, however, to read the small print on the chart, and Captain Regnier, breathing short and heavily with the exertion of moving his vast shapeless form, lighted the lamp. My feebleness would not suffer me to rise and bend over the chart, and perceiving this the two Frenchmen held open before me the wide sheet of cartridge paper.

'There,' said Captain Regnier, pointing to a part of the chart with a large fat forefinger on which glittered a thick silver ring, 'there,' said he, 'is the situation of *Notre Dame de Boulogne* at the present moment.'

'That point of land,' exclaimed Alphonse after translating, 'is Finisterre. The brick then is off Finisterre. Does the name of Finisterre give you any ideas?'

I continued to think, with my eyes rooted to the chart, and then I answered, 'None.'

'Here is Toulon,' said Captain Regnier, 'and this is the course of the vessel to that port,' and he ran his fat finger down the chart, past the coast of Spain and through the Straits of Gibraltar to the Gulf of Lyons.

'It is a long way to Toulon,' said I.

'Yes,' answered Alphonse, 'it is a voyage.'

Captain Regnier addressed his nephew. 'Superb! Admirable!' cried the young Frenchman. 'Ah, my uncle is a clever man! What do you think he proposes? That you shall look at the coast of England and read the names upon it, and if you are an English lady who, as my uncle says, has been blown away in a pleasure-boat from a port in England, why——' and with great excitement he pulled the end of the chart out of his uncle's hand, rolled it up until only that portion which contained the English Channel was left open, and then placed the chart thus rolled up upon my knees.

I looked, and the two Frenchmen stood viewing me. I trembled with eagerness and fear, for I thought to myself, 'Here may be the spark that will flash up the whole of the blackened galleries of my memory—and yet it may not be here!' and shiver after shiver ran through me as I looked.

'Read aloud, madame; read aloud,' exclaimed Alphonse.

I read aloud; name after name I pronounced, taking the towns one after the other, from the Thames to the Land's End, and then with trembling finger and whispering lips I traced the coast on the western side, even to the height of Scotland; and then I continued to read down on the eastern coast until I came to the River Thames.

'Ah, my God! my God!' I cried, and I hid my eyes and sobbed. The chart rolled from my knees on to the deck.

'Patience,' exclaimed Captain Regnier. 'The memory will return. Give her some wine, Alphonse.'

I drank, but though I recovered my composure there had happened such a deadly struggle within me, so fierce and rending a conflict—betwixt, what shall I say? the spirit, shall I call it, grappling with eyeless memory?—that I lay back in my chair, prostrated, incapable of speech. And how am I to convey to you, who are following my story, the effect produced by the words I read—by the names of the towns I read aloud—upon my mind? This was the difficulty I foresaw when I undertook to relate my experiences. But let me do my best. The effect was this: the names I uttered—that is to say, the names of those towns which I had heard of; for some little places which I had never heard of were marked upon the chart—the names, then, of places which I had heard of and known sounded as familiarly to my ear as my own name would have sounded before my memory went. But that was all. I could associate no ideas with them. They presented no images. They were perfectly familiar *sounds* and no more. Though the chart was of French, or at all events of foreign manufacture, all names in Great Britain were printed as they are spelt by us. Therefore I could not console myself with reflecting that the words I had read were spelt in the French way, and without suggestion to one whose memory was gone. No, every word was in English. Often have I since wondered whether Piertown was included in that chart. Probably it was not. So insignificant a place would not be deemed worth marking down.

'The lady is undoubtedly English,' said Captain Regnier to his nephew. 'Only a native of her country could pronounce its tongue as she does.'

'I am not so sure of that,' answered Alphonse. 'I have known Germans and Danes, and I have known Dutchmen and Swedes who have spoken English as well as madame. Uncle, I know a thing or two. Be a waiter and you will learn much to astonish you. But I agree that she is an Englishwoman, yet not because she speaks English well. Her style is English, and you will find that she is a lady of rank.'

This conversation I was able to imperfectly follow. I felt too ill, too miserably sick at heart to sit in that cabin conversing, and begged Alphonse to conduct me to my berth. He did so with the same gentleness and courteous attention with which he had led me from it. Before leaving me he said, 'If it is fine to-morrow I shall have the pleasure to take you on deck. The fresh air will do you a great deal of good. And, who knows? your memory doubtless left you while you were in the boat. It is, therefore, in the sea, and when you look at the sea it may come up to you out of it.'

I enjoyed some hours' sleep that night and awoke refreshed and stronger. I tried to remember if I had dreamt. Before I fell asleep it entered my head to fancy that if I dreamt of even a little bit of my past—that even if in a vision, the merest corner of the black curtain would rise to enable me to catch a glimpse of what was behind when I awoke—then by remembering *that* I should end in remembering all. But when I tried to think if I had dreamt I found that my slumber had been without visions. I dwelt upon those dark hours of sleep, but they had been dreamless, and there was nothing to evoke.

It was a fine bright morning. The vessel was sailing along almost upright, with a regular succession of floating falls and risings of that hinder part of her in which my berth was situated. The glory of the ocean morning was upon the waters; they flashed in blueish silver windily, and the dazzle rising off them streamed in trembling splendour through the porthole, and filled the little coarse and homely berth with ripples of lustre.

Alphonse brought me some soup, biscuit, and a new-laid egg from the hencoop in which were stocked the few hens which the brig carried. When I had finished the repast I arose and dressed myself, and entered the cabin or living-room, where sat Alphonse playing the fiddle, whilst the mate, Hénin, seated on one of the chests or lockers, with half a tumbler of claret in one hand and a biscuit in the other, kept time by nodding.

'Very good, indeed, madame; very good, indeed!' cried Alphonse, putting his fiddle down and clapping his hands. 'I did not believe you would get up until the afternoon. Come! you are better, and you will be well before we arrive at Toulon, where you will find your memory waiting for you.'

'I do not understand,' exclaimed the fierce-looking mate Hénin, staring at me with gleaming eyes, though he addressed Alphonse and spoke in French, 'why it is that the lady does not remember. Can she recollect yesterday? Undoubtedly,' he exclaimed with a savage gesture. 'Then the brain that can recall yesterday should be able to bring back as many yesterdays as it needs. Let the lady try, and she will remember.'

'Bah!' said Alphonse. 'Do not mind this man,' said he. 'He does not understand English, and I can say what I like. Do not suppose him fierce because he looks so. He has a tender heart, and weeps easily. Yet there is not a more excellent sailor in the French marine; at least my uncle says so, and my uncle is a very clever man. Shall I now conduct you on deck?'

'I should like to go on deck,' said I.

'Let me see; you will want a chair. You are not yet able to stand long or walk very far, and you have no covering for your head.'

I put my hand to my hair and exclaimed, 'Was I without covering to my head when you found me?'

'No. You wore a straw hat. It was crushed by the fall of the mast. When the sailors raised you to bring you on board, the hat fell off, and they left it in the boat. One of the men in the bad light saw a dark mark upon the straw, and he said it might be blood.'

'It was a straw hat?' said I. 'A straw hat?' and I mused until I began to *think* myself into one of those black and frightful conflicts of mind which had before prostrated me with their unspeakable anguish. I checked the horrible internal struggle by forcing myself to speak, and so diverting my thoughts.

'What is there that I can wear to protect my head?'

The mate Hénin, who continued to stare at me with fiery eyes, said, 'What does the lady say?' Alphonse explained. 'Wait,' cried Hénin fiercely, and, putting down his glass and biscuit, he went to the ring in the forward wall of the cabin, slid the door open, and disappeared. In a minute he returned with a long cloak hanging over his arm. He ran his eye over my figure, then held up the cloak to compute its size. It was a dark green cloak, of a very monkish pattern; it had a large hood, and was comfortably lined with some sort of delicate fur.

'Let the lady wear this,' exclaimed the man. 'It is almost new, and therefore clean. She is welcome to it,' and he flung it into the outstretched hands of Alphonse, and, with a fierce countenance, resumed his seat.

I put on the cloak; it was loose, and completely enveloped me. I then drew the hood over my head, and, assisted by the young Frenchman, painfully ascended the steep steps and gained the deck. The first sweep of the fresh sunlit wind almost overpowered me; I reeled and closed my eyes, but this swooning sensation speedily passed.

The huge fat figure of Captain Regnier stood near the wheel; Alphonse called to him to give me the support of his arm until the chair was brought on deck. After the comparative gloom of the cabin the brilliant morning sunshine nearly blinded me, and for some while I was forced to keep my eyes half closed. In a few moments Alphonse came up the stairs with the armchair, which he placed in the sunshine, but in a part of the deck that was sheltered from the wind by the box or hood that was fitted over the little hatch that conducted to the cabin. And now, my sight having grown used to the dazzle, I looked about me.

I found myself on the deck of a small vessel, whose shape resembled that of a box rather than that of a ship. She had two masts, across which were stretched sheets of patched and discoloured canvas. On the top of the hinder mast was a small red streamer, surmounted by a little brass ship that shone like a ray of white fire in the air as it pointed with its red streamer attached directly in the path along which the brig was being steered. The planks of the deck were dark, and every object that the eye rested upon suggested dirt and neglect. I remarked a boat painted white standing upside down near a little wooden house like a sentry-box, whose roof was pierced by a chimney from which a trail of dark smoke was blowing over the bows. I gazed earnestly at that boat; it seemed a familiar object to me; all else was strange—the tall masts, the wide-spread sails, the straight black lines of rigging, the dingy green paint of the bulwarks, the twenty details of rope hanging in coils, of pumps, of skylight, and I know not what else, for how should a woman be able to give names to the strange furniture of the sea? All else was new. I searched my dark mind, and the picture of this brig sailing along with the wind blowing over her stern into her dingy wings was as novel as though she were the only vessel in the world, and I was beholding her for the first time.

But the boat seemed familiar. I could not take my eyes off it for some minutes. Why should this be? I asked; and then my sightless memory began to struggle, and I addressed the young Frenchman, who stood at my side, for the relief to be found in speech.

'I seem to have seen that boat before.'

'Impossible, madame.'

'What does the lady say?' exclaimed Captain Regnier, who leaned against the bulwarks with his hands in his pockets opposite me.

Alphonse repeated my words. The large fat man pulled one hand out of his pocket to emphasise his speech with gestures.

'My uncle says no. You cannot remember that boat,' said the young Frenchman. 'He has owned this brick twenty years, and the boat is twenty years old, and in all that time she has belonged to the brick.'

'Why, then, should she seem familiar to me?'

He reflected, and then put his forefinger to the side of his nose.

'I think I know. We took you out of a boat; all your sufferings were in a boat; the idea of a boat has been burnt in upon your mind by pain and misery; and now when you see a boat you cry out—"Ah! surely I know her." You will say that of any boat. It is a very good sign. I say it is a very good sign that you should think you know that boat.'

He then volubly addressed his uncle, who nodded, and grunted, and shrugged, and appeared to agree.

I remarked two or three men about the deck in the fore-part of the brig. They were ill-clad, lean and yellow, and grim, dark and forbidding for want of the razor. They stared very hard at me, ceasing in their work to do so, and certainly their curiosity was more than justified, for I can well believe that I made an extraordinary figure with my plaistered and withered face, and white hair showing in the twilight of the large hood, and the rest of me draped by the cloak to the very plank of the deck.

It was a beautiful morning, the hour about eleven. The ocean was of the colour of sapphire, and it flowed with the brig in long and regular lines, and here and there the froth fitfully flashed and faded. The sky on the left was shaded with a high delicate network of cloud, but elsewhere the firmament was of purest blue, graced and relieved by widely scattered little bodies of pearl-like vapour, all sailing our way. The wind was sweet and mild, and now every breath that I took of it seemed to give me a new spirit.

'Look there, madame,' exclaimed Alphonse, 'you have not yet seen that beautiful sight,' and directing my eyes over the bulwark on the right, I beheld a stately ship, a large, lovely, and radiant fabric, with sail upon sail of the milk-white softness of sifted snow swelling and diminishing one above another to an altitude that made one think of the little gold buttons on the top of her masts as stars. She was passing us swiftly. A small white line of foam throbbed along the long red streak that rose up her side a little above the level of the water. Soft flames of white fire broke from many parts of her as she swept her windows and the glass upon the deck and many ornaments of furniture of polished brass into the direct flash of the sun.

'Oh! that is a beautiful sight, indeed,' said I.

'Does it give you no idea, madame?' said the young Frenchman; then finding that I continued to gaze without answering him, he exclaimed: 'Look now at the sea. Is there not something in the sight of that sea to make you remember? Figure land yonder, and imagine for yourself a town upon it. What sort of town shall it be? Come, it must be the town you sailed from in the boat with two masts. And see now if we cannot create it. It will have a pier—there will be sands: or say it has no pier, and the cliffs are white——'

'Oh God, my heart will break,' I cried.

Another day and yet another day passed. And now I had been a little longer than a week on board the French brig.

It was Sunday. The day had broken in gloom, and when I arose and dressed myself at ten o'clock I could scarcely see in my cabin. There did not seem to be any wind. The vessel was rolling somewhat heavily, and alternately she plunged the circular window of my cabin under water, and then the dusk turned black with nothing but a green glimmer where the porthole was; and then as she rolled away on the other side and lifted the little window weeping and roaring out of the swollen hill of green water, there was a noise as of the explosion of guns; but no foam flew about the window, whence I judged that the vessel was not making any progress.

By this time I had grown accustomed to the motions of a ship at sea. I moved without difficulty, and poised myself to the slanting of the deck under my feet with something of the ease of habit. When I had dressed myself on this Sunday morning I put on the cloak that the mate Hénin had lent me, and entered the little state cabin or living room. The young Frenchman, Alphonse, sat at the table with an open volume before him. He looked up as I approached.

'Well,' said he, 'is it as bad as you feared?'

'Yes,' I answered; 'if my hair goes on falling out as it now does, I shall be bald before we arrive at Toulon.'

He smiled and said: 'Oh no! You have a great deal of hair. Many ladies have I seen, but never one with such abundance of hair as you.'

'I am losing it fast.'

'It will grow again. It is not as if you were very old.'

'Very old!' I exclaimed, 'what is my age? What do you think it is? Tell me. I earnestly wish to guess.' Then, observing a certain expression to enter his face, I added with vehemence: 'Do not attempt to flatter me. Tell me exactly what you believe my age to be. Even out of *that* may come an idea to me.'

'It would not be fair to you to guess,' said the young man, with the little French smirk that had entered his face swiftly fading out of it; 'look how your forehead is bound up! Figure yourself in good health—your face entirely visible—*bien coiffée* besides—but you ask me for the truth, and I will tell you what I suppose. You are, madame, about forty-five years old.'

'It may be so,' I answered, and my head sank, and for some moments my senses seemed to leave me, so benumbing was the bewilderment that possessed me as I tried to think, wondering why I could not remember my age, wondering why I could not remember my name, wondering whether the sable curtain before which the hand of calamity had placed me would ever rise.

'The French,' said Alphonse, 'are hair-dressers in perfection. There is a hair-dresser of genius at Toulon. He is my friend. I will speak to him, and it will be strange if he does not possess the secret of preventing your hair from falling out.' He closed his book and continued: 'I believe you will not much longer require to wear that plaister, yet I would advise you to keep it on until you are able to consult a physician. A friend of mine at Toulon is an excellent doctor. I will speak to him about you. But how gloomy—how gloomy is this day! I hope there will not be a storm. Would you like to go on deck?'

I mounted the steps and looked about me. The scene of ocean was indeed a melancholy one. The sea was running in large heaps of ugly green, and there was not a breath of air to wrinkle the polished slopes. The sky was a wide and sullen shadow of grey, nowhere broken, and the sweeping folds of the water worked and throbbed all round the base of that mighty stretch of shadow as though they washed the foot of a vast circular wall. The vessel rolled from side to side, and at times her canvas slapped the mast with a noise like a sudden clap of thunder. At a distance lay a ship rigged as ours was. She had very little canvas set, but what she showed was white, and it glared out like the breaking head of a sea as she swayed her masts.

Mate Hénin was on deck. He stood at the bulwark, and supported his rocking figure by holding a rope, and the scowl upon his face as he ran his gleaming eyes over the sea was as dark as the scowl upon the sky.

'How is this weather to end?' called Alphonse to him.

'In wind,' he answered.

'Will it be a fair wind?'

'The devil alone knows. But better a hurricane than this.' He uttered a malediction. 'Is it to be Toulon with us? Or is it to be six months of the Bay of Biscay? Are we to run short of water and provisions? I am no oyster, I. Give me a hurricane sooner than six months of the Bay of Biscay in this tumbling shell.' He uttered another malediction, and scowled even yet more fiercely as he looked up at the sky and then around him.

Alphonse translated his speech with a smile. 'Do not mind him,' he exclaimed; 'he has a tender heart and no man sheds tears more easily.'

It began to rain and I returned to the cabin. I removed the cloak, seated myself on a locker and gave myself up to thought. If I could not remember who I was, what was to become of me? When this brig arrived at Toulon whither should I proceed for shelter and protection? Captain Regnier had spoken of the British Consul; but I was a stranger to the British Consul. I had nothing whatever to communicate to him about my past, saving that I was found far out at sea in a little sailing-boat, and rescued by the people of the brig *Notre Dame de Boulogne*. Would he house me or elsewhere find shelter and food for me until he had discovered who I was? But how would he be able to discover who I was? And when he found that inquiry was futile would he go on sheltering and protecting me? My thoughts filled me with terror. I was ignorant of the duties of a Consul, and I could not understand that there might be anything to hope or to expect from him. Then, again, my memory being gone, I was as much at fault when I reasoned forwards as when I directed the eyes of my mind backwards. I could not conceive, for instance, that on my landing at Toulon, and representing my dreadful and helpless condition to the British Consul, he would take steps to send me home, because I had no imagination of home. I could not positively affirm that I was English; I was in the condition of a mute—nay, I was far worse off than a mute, because a mute has his memory, and can express what is in his mind by writing or by dumb show; whereas I had nothing to tell. I could speak, and the words I pronounced were English; but that was all. However my tale might run, it would be without meaning: and when I thought of myself as landing at Toulon, of arriving at a place where I had not a friend—though if there had been twenty friends there I should not have remembered them—when I thought of the few shillings my purse contained, that all the wearing apparel I possessed was upon me, that I should not be able to say who I was, where I came from, in what part of the world my home was situated—when I thought thus I trembled in every limb, my heart felt cold as stone, and I strove to ease the agony of my mind by weeping; but no tears flowed. I had wept so often of late throughout the days, and in the dark hours of the nights, that the source of my tears seemed to have been dried up.

The good-natured Alphonse, observing the dreadful and insupportable misery in my face and posture, thought to cheer me up; he sat beside me, entreated me not to fret, and spoke cheerfully of the future. But my inward anguish was too extreme to suffer me to listen to him, and after awhile he withdrew to his cabin and played somewhat stealthily upon his fiddle, thinking, perhaps, I could not hear him, yet wishing to divert himself.

Shortly before the cabin dinner hour, that is to say, a little before one o'clock, there was a sudden commotion on deck, a noise of ropes hastily flung down, the sounds of men running about, accompanied by Captain Regnier's bull-like bawlings. In a few minutes I heard a strange hissing, and the vessel leaned over and continued to lean down until she had arrived at so sharp an angle that I was only saved from sliding off the locker by pressing at the whole length of my arms against the table. The shouts of the men on deck were confused and incessant. Every man seemed to be roaring out orders on his own account. There was likewise an alarming noise of canvas violently shaken. The vessel was plunging heavily, and every now and then she received a blow from a sea that thrilled through her as a house shakes when a loaded van is passing the door, and every blow was followed by a fierce noise of seething like the sound of water poured on fire.

The young Frenchman's cabin door opened and Alphonse crawled out on his hands and knees. He climbed up the slope of the deck to the side of the table at which I sat, and gazed at me with an ashen countenance.

'This is terrible!' he cried.

'What has happened?' I asked.

'A frightful storm has burst upon us!' he answered. 'Blessed Virgin! why does not the brick lift herself out of the water?' and here he made the sign of the Cross upon his breast, which led me to suppose that, like many other Frenchmen, and like many other people who are not Frenchmen, Alphonse was an infidel only in fine weather.

We remained seated, hearkening with terrified ears to the uproar on deck and to the thunderous beating of the sea against the little vessel. After some while the brig grew more upright, the halloaing above ceased, and there was nothing to be heard save the creaking of the old structure as it pitched and wallowed, and a subdued noise of angry, raving, foaming waters.

The light in the hatchway was eclipsed, and the immense mass of Captain Regnier descended the steps. His coat was streaming, and on his gaining the cabin he pulled off his sodden red cap and flung it with a furious gesture into a corner.

'Oh, uncle, what is the matter?' cried Alphonse, clasping his hands.

'Matter!' answered Captain Regnier, 'why here is a dead foul wind blowing strong enough, if it lasts for twenty-four hours, to lose us every league we have gained in the last three days.'

'Is there any danger?' asked Alphonse.

The large fat man eyed him in silence for a moment, then, pulling a big silver watch from the waistband of his trousers, he roared out: 'Let us dine or there will be plenty of danger.'

This said he ascended the steps until his head was in the air above the cover, and having delivered himself of a bull-like shout he returned, pulled off his great overcoat, and seated himself in his shabby velveteen jacket.

'But you will tell me if there is any danger?' said Alphonse.

'I will tell you nothing until I have dined,' answered Captain Regnier.

The young man sat with a white face viewing his uncle wistfully. There was expression enough in the fat Frenchman's stolid face to reassure me; moreover, I could not suppose that he would think of his dinner and apparently of nothing but his dinner in a time of danger. Yet, had he informed Alphonse that the brig was in peril I should have listened to the news with indifference. My dejection was heart-crushing. I was wretched to the inmost recesses of my spirit with the despair that comes of hopelessness, and never before had I felt so lonely.

The brig's movements were horribly uncomfortable. It was blowing very hard and the sea was growing. I do not know whether the vessel was sailing—that is to say, whether she was making any progress through the water—but they were steering her so as to cause her side to form an angle with the gulfs of the foaming billows, and the dance of the light structure was as though she must at any moment go to pieces.

Despite the jerky, convulsive, dislocating movements, the grimy French lad who waited in the cabin contrived to place the dinner upon the table. The meal was composed largely of soup, and I cannot conceive how the youth managed. I drank a little soup and ate a piece of biscuit, and this with a small draught of red wine formed my dinner. Alphonse ate nothing; he continuously gazed at his uncle, who addressed himself to the meal with both hands, gradually lying back as he drained the contents of a large tin dishful of soup, and then placing a bottle half full of wine at his lips and emptying it, and then grasping a large piece of sausage with one hand and a whole biscuit with the other and rapidly devouring them.

'This is not a moment to think of knives and forks,' said he; 'if we are to perish let us meet our end well lined.'

'To perish!' cried Alphonse.

'Bah!' exclaimed Captain Regnier, with his mouth full. 'Did you not tell me the other day that if I were a waiter I would know a thing or two? Well, I now imagine myself a waiter, and am talking as one. As a waiter I pronounce that we shall perish, but as a sailor I say no! no! we shall not perish this time. There are many napkins remaining for you to fashion into fans and cocked-hats before you are drowned by shipwreck.'

The young Frenchman's vivacity immediately returned to him.

'It is inspiriting to even think of napkins at such a time,' said he. 'They awaken fancies of the hotel, the *table-d'hôte*, of a thousand agreeable things. After Toulon—the deluge. You do not catch me returning to Boulogne with you, uncle. Give me the railway. I now detest the sea. Ciel! how the ship leaps. And remark this poor lady. How has the sea served her?' He snapped his fingers, and extended his hand for a piece of the sausage.

Both men spoke in French, but I understood enough of their discourse to enable me to repeat the substance of it.

'If this wind holds,' said Captain Regnier, 'it will be the deluge before Toulon. A thousand thunders! To think that it should come on to storm dead ahead! What virtue is there in patience when there is no end to waiting?'

'Why not sail the ship to a convenient port,' said Alphonse, 'and wait there in comfort and serenity until the weather changes?'

'Go! you are a sot,' responded Captain Regnier, scowling at him.

The motion was so excessive that it pained me to sit upright. I spoke to Alphonse, who addressed his uncle, and the captain, going to my berth, brought the mattress from the sleeping shelf, and placed it on one of the chests or lockers on what is called the 'lee side'—that is, on the depressed side of the vessel—and when he had fetched the bolster I lay down.

The afternoon slowly passed away. The skylight was shrouded with wet, and the shadow of the storm-coloured sky was upon it, and in the cabin it was so gloomy that Alphonse told the lad who waited at table to light the lamp. I was not sea-sick, but the swift risings and fallings of the brig gave me a dreadful headache, and so dimmed my sight that I could scarcely see.

You who read this may very well know the sea as it is to be experienced in large ships. You may have rolled and plunged over mountainous waves in a steam-vessel of vast bulk, whose cabin is radiant with mirrors and lamps of polished metal, and with furniture as sumptuous as that of the drawing-rooms of a palace! You have had a luxurious berth to withdraw to, attentive stewards or stewardesses to minister to you, and all the while you have been comforted with a sense of incessant progress, with the assurance of the pulse in everything that you touch, in everything that you feel, that the noble engines are magnificently doing their work, and ruthlessly forcing the crushing and shearing stem of the powerful metal structure along the path that leads to your destination.

But exchange such a ship as this for a brig of small burthen; exchange the brilliant interior of the great ship for the dingy, snuff-coloured living-room of a little brig with scarcely light to see by, and with the air full of the thunder of the warring without. Often the lamp swung so violently under the beam from which it dangled that I languidly watched to see it extinguish its own flame against the upper decks. There was a sickening sound of sobbing waters over my head, and there were many furious discharges of spray or wet upon the planks, the noise of which was like the abrupt fall of a terrible hailstorm liberated from the black breast of a tropical electric cloud.

The afternoon passed and the evening came, and when Captain Regnier descended from the deck to eat his supper he told his nephew, who had hidden himself in his berth during the afternoon, that the weather was moderating, and that, though he expected the night would be very dark, the wind would enable him to make sail. It befel as he had predicted. By seven o'clock the wind was no more than what sailors would term a moderate breeze, and the sea was fast going down, though at this hour the brig was still plunging heavily. It was pitch dark, however, on deck. When the mate Hénin came into the cabin to fetch a warm coat to keep his watch in, or, in other words, to wear whilst he took charge of the brig from eight o'clock until some late hour of the night, he addressed a number of sentences with great vehemence and impetuosity to the young Frenchman, who, on the mate withdrawing, informed me that Hénin declared that in twenty-eight years' experience of the sea he had never remembered such blackness as was at this time upon the ocean.

'Would you believe it, madame?' cried Alphonse. 'Hénin swears that the very foam which breaks close alongside the brick is not to be seen. What do you think of that?—I will go and look at the night for myself.'

He ascended the steps, but speedily returned. 'It is raining,' said he, 'and it is cold too, I can tell you. And does Hénin call it black? Black is too weak a word. I will tell you what it is like: it is like the blackness of a stormy night, when you look at it after your eyes have been fearfully dazzled by a flash of lightning.'

All this while I remained extended upon the mattress upon the locker, covered by mate Hénin's cloak, and with head pillowed on the rude bolster that had been withdrawn from my sleeping-shelf. Soon after the mate had gone on deck, Captain Regnier came down the stairs. He took his seat at the table under the lamp, and Alphonse produced a box of dominos. The captain, who on a previous occasion had learnt that I did not object to the smell of tobacco, filled a strange pipe formed of a great Turk's head and a long curved stem, and smoked. He likewise put his hand into an adjacent locker and mixed himself a tumbler of white liquor which, that it might not upset, he placed upon a small tray that was oscillating above the table. The two men then played with singular gravity, the fat man smoking with stolid deliberation, whilst the young man watched the game with impassioned intentness.

The little brig groaned and pitched and tossed; the skylight glass overhead lay in panes of ebony, and duskily and gleamingly reflected the figures of the two domino players; through the open hatch that conducted to the deck came the roaring and hissing noise of conflicting waters and the whistling of the wind in the rigging. It was raining hard; the rain-drops lashed the glass of the skylight. I gazed at the two men, but I did not know that I watched them. All the while I was asking myself, What can the letters 'A. C.' stand for? And I tried to recollect the names of women, but in vain. Then I said to myself, Am I English, or is it likely that the young Frenchman was right when he said that I might be a German who spoke English with a perfect accent, and who now, by some caprice of the reason cruelly afflicted by suffering, is compelled to speak in the English tongue, forgetting her own?

Many extraordinary thoughts or fancies of this kind visited me as I lay watching those two domino players. Imagine yourself without memory, not merely unable to recollect in this or in that direction: no. But imagine your mind without power to suggest a single idea to you, to submit a single image to you that had existence previous to an hour comparatively recent!

At nine o'clock I withdrew to my berth. By this hour the two men had finished with their dominos. Alphonse replaced the mattress and bolster in my sleeping-shelf, and whilst he was thus occupied I said to him: 'I feel a strange horror upon me to-night. There is a sense of loneliness in me that seems to be breaking my heart.'

'Madame must cheer up. She will find her memory at Toulon.'

'My mind is hopelessly dark and silent. I have been all this evening trying to think, and the struggle has made me ill.'

'I will fetch you some brandy and water.'

'No, thank you. What you gave me half an hour ago is sufficient. It is not that—I dread the darkness of the long night—the fearful solitude—oh, the fearful solitude! Will not Captain Regnier permit me to burn a light.'

'He is timid, and very properly timid,' answered Alphonse. 'Conceive a fire breaking out. A fire at sea, and on such a night as this!' He shuddered, and then looked up at the strange globular lamp that depended from the centre of the ceiling of my cabin. We conversed with the door open, and the lamp that burned in the living room shed a faint light upon the interior of my berth. 'But it *is* lonely,' the young Frenchman continued in a voice of pity. 'I dare say my uncle will not mind—at all events he need not know.' He raised his hand to the lamp, and with a twist removed the metal bowl or compartment for the oil and mesh out of the globe. 'I will fill this, and bring it back to you,' said he.

He returned after a short absence, lighted the wick, and turned it down that it might burn dimly, then screwed it into the globe. I felt deeply grateful, and took his hand and held it whilst I thanked him. He left me, and putting on mate Hénin's cloak to keep me warm, I got into my miserable little sleeping shelf and lay down, grateful for, and feeling even soothed by, being able to see.

CHAPTER VI
A TERRIBLE NIGHT

I MAY have slept for an hour or two; but for the light of the lamp, I believe, I should not have closed my eyes in rest, so unendurable would my spirits have found the heavy burthen of the darkness of the night. I opened my eyes. The lamp burned dimly. The vessel was rolling somewhat briskly, and I seemed to hear a louder noise of wind than I had noticed before falling asleep. The creaking throughout the cabin was ceaseless and distracting. The rudder jarred heavily upon its hinges, and every time a billow smote it I felt a shock as though the brig had struck on a rock.

On a sudden I heard a cry. It came faint and weak to my ears through the deck and through the door; but I heard it, and I caught the note of horror in it, and never shall I forget that cry! Whenever I recall it I think of the wailing scream of some strange wild tropic beast, wounded to the death and faltering to the edge of a river, and there sending its death cry into the quiet Indian night.

The sound was re-echoed over my head, followed by a hasty rush of feet. A few moments later there was a terrific blow. The concussion was as though the brig had blown up. I heard the rending and smashing and splintering noises of falling masts and of bulwarks crushed. The brig heeled over and over, and yet over; one might have supposed that some mighty hand had grasped her side and was slowly swaying and pressing her upside down. Fortunately for me the wild and inexpressible slope of the vessel to one side laid me against the wall to which my sleeping-shelf was fixed, and so I could not fall out. Had it been the other way about I must certainly have been flung from my bed, when, in all probability, I should have broken a limb if not my neck.

Whilst the brig was in the act of heeling over, something heavy immediately outside my berth gave way, struck the door, which, opening outwards, was not burst, though the blow it received might well have demolished the whole of the wooden wall in which the door was hung. I tried to get out of the sleeping-shelf, but the slope continued so sharp that I could not stir. There were many noises, but my cabin was situated in the stern of the brig, and the confused sounds reached my ears dully. When the vessel leaned over immediately after she had been struck, the cargo in the hold gave way, raising an instant's thunder of rattling and clattering, and shaking the whole structure to its heart. I strained my ears for human voices, but caught but a dim far-away shout or two. I could not get out of my sleeping-shelf, and, believing that the brig was sinking, I screamed to the young Frenchman, who I supposed was in the next cabin, but got no answer. I screamed again and yet again, but no reply was returned.

What had happened? Ignorant as I was of the sea, how could I imagine what had happened? Was Captain Regnier wholly wrong in his calculations, and had he run his brig ashore? The sea was leaping angrily over the sloping side in which the little porthole of my cabin was fixed. It broke over the window as though the hull of the brig had been an immovable rock, and every billow roared and hissed as it fell back after its furious leap shattered and boiling. Presently the vessel regained a somewhat upright posture, but her movements were terribly staggering. She rose and fell, and rolled from side to side convulsively. She appeared to be labouring in the heart of an angry sea that was ridging towards her from all points of the compass.

I was almost out of my mind with terror, and the moment the decreased slope of the brig enabled me to stir, I sprang from my shelf, and hastily putting on the few articles of raiment which I had removed, and clothing myself in mate Hénin's cloak, I made for the door, too terrified to appreciate the blessing of having a light to see by or to guess what my sensations would have been had the berth been in darkness. I grasped the handle of the door, but the door would not open. I pushed it with all my might, but it would not stir an inch. I looked to see if, when I turned the handle, the latch shot back. Yes! the latch shot back, and if it depended upon the handle, the door was to be easily opened. Something pressed against it outside, something that would not yield by the fraction of an inch though I pushed with the strength of frenzy.

I continued to push and to scream until I was seized with faintness; my arms sank to my side and my knees gave way. Oh! am I to be left to drown, locked up in this berth? I cried to myself, and I reeled to the arm-chair and sat down in it incapable of standing.

The noise caused by the lashing of the sea just outside and the sounds of cargo rolling about in the hold overwhelmed all that I might else have heard sounding from above. Whilst I sat panting and half-swooning a man cried out at my door.

'Oh, help me! help me!' I shrieked, and new strength coming to me with the sound of his voice, I staggered to my feet.

'Oh my God!' cried the voice of Alphonse in French, 'I cannot move this cask. Help! help!'

Then I could hear the voice of Captain Regnier roaring in the distance as though he had put his head into the hatchway and was crying to his nephew through it.

'Oh, Alphonse, release me, save me, I cannot open the door!' I shrieked.

He answered in a voice of agony, but what he said I could not catch, and this was followed by a sound of furious wrestling outside. Another wild and frantic cry from Captain Regnier rang through the cabin, and now the words uttered at the top of his powerful voice reached me. They were, 'If you do not come instantly we must leave you behind to perish.' Again I caught a noise of desperate wrestling. It ceased.

'Oh, Alphonse, do not leave me!' I screamed. 'Do not leave me to be drowned in this dreadful berth!' and I strained my ears but I heard nothing to tell me that the young Frenchman was outside; nevertheless I stood listening, supporting my tottering and swaying figure by holding to the handle of the door, for though I had heard his uncle call to him to hasten on deck or he would be left to perish, I could not believe that he would leave me to drown—that Alphonse would abandon me to a dreadful fate though all the others should quit the brig. I thought to myself, he has rushed on deck to remonstrate with Captain Regnier; he is now imploring his uncle and the others to descend and help him to remove the cask and liberate me, for I had heard him exclaim that the door was blocked by a cask, and I recollected that one immense cask or barrel had stood under the ladder which conducted to the deck; and remembering this I supposed that when the brig had violently leaned over, the cask had torn itself from its fastenings and been hurled by the slant of the deck against the door of my berth, where it lay jammed, immovably holding the door.

I stood listening, I say, but the minutes passed and I heard nothing—nothing, I mean, that resembled a human voice or the movements of men; otherwise there was no lack of sounds—horrible, dismal, affrighting noises, a ceaseless thumping as of wreckage pounding against the sides of the brig, a muffled, most melancholy whistling and wailing of wind, a constant rattle and roar of cargo in the hold, a frequent shock of sea smiting the window of my cabin and filling the air with a sharp hissing and boiling, as of the foot of a great cataract.

But when, after waiting and listening, I began to understand that Alphonse had fled with the rest, that there was nobody in the brig to come to my assistance, that I was imprisoned in a cell from which I could not break out and which might be slowly settling under water even as I stood, then was I maddened by an agony of fear and horror. I uttered shriek after shriek; I dashed at the door with my shoulder; I wept, and cowering to the chair sank upon it; then I shrieked again, and falling on my knees upon the chair I buried my face and lay motionless.

I lay motionless, and after many minutes had passed I lifted up my head and gazed round the cabin, and a feeling of calmness suddenly settled upon my spirits. Whence came that feeling of calmness? Not surely from any faint hope that my life would yet be preserved, because I had not the least doubt that the vessel was sinking and that the final plunge must happen at the next moment or the next. The feeling of calmness came from the Spirit of God. From what other source could it proceed? But it never occurred to me that the Spirit of God was present in that little berth; it never occurred to me to pray to Him for succour, or, seeing that I was convinced I was a dying woman, to pray to Him to make my last struggles easy and to forgive me for my past, whatever it might hold—for hidden as that past was, it was human, and must therefore need forgiveness. It could not occur to me to pray, because I was without memory and my mind was unable to suggest the thought of God. But as though I had prayed and as though my prayer had been answered my mind grew tranquil.

I arose and seated myself afresh in the chair, and clasping my hands and leaning back my head I fixed my eyes on the lamp for the comfort of the companionship of the little flame in it. My intelligence was horribly active, but the singular tranquillity within me was not to be disturbed by the most dreadful of the imaginations which arose. I remember that I calmly figured the moment when the brig would sink, and I imagined a noise of thunder as the water roared in through the hatchways; and then I had a fancy of the water taking a long while to drain into the stoutly-enclosed berth, and of my sitting and watching the flood slowly rising, washing in foam from side to side to the rolling of the brig, but steadily rising nevertheless. All this I figured, and many more frightful pictures passed before my inner vision. Yet I continued calm and sat waiting for my end, supported by a strength that had come to me without a prayer.

The hours passed and the brig still lived, and still did I remain seated awaiting the moment that I believed inevitable. No stupor was upon me: I took heed of what was passing. I remarked that the brig rolled more gently, that the seas lashed my cabin windows less spitefully, that the dreary pounding as of wreckage smiting the side penetrated the fabric with a more softened note.

At last, turning my eyes in the direction of the window, I observed that the gleaming ebony of it had changed into a faint green, and it glimmered now as it had glimmered on that morning when I first opened my eyes on board the brig. I knew that the storm had broken; but if the vessel had been deserted by her crew, what would daylight signify to me, who was locked up in a little berth, the sole living creature on board a wreck— as I *knew* the brig to be—which passing vessels would glance at without visiting, and which could not much longer remain afloat?

I watched the disk of glass change from dim green into clear yellow, and whilst I continued to gaze, I heard a sound resembling the voice of a man outside. Before I could make sure that it had been a human voice, I heard it again. It was the voice of a man calling to another. My strength returned to me as though I had been electrified, and springing to my feet I rushed to the door and beat upon it. I smote the door with all my strength with both hands clenched, and shrieked 'Help! help! Save me! Release me!' in notes preternaturally shrill with the maddening excitement of the tremendous hope and the desperate fears which possessed me. In a moment the door was thumped outside, and a man called out:

'All right! we'll see to you—we'll release you;' and then I heard him shout in a roar that was even louder than the bull-like tones of Captain Regnier, 'Wilkins, there's a woman locked up here. For God's sake bear a hand and jump on deck, and bring a couple of hands out of the boat to clear away this cask. Here's a cask that's gone adrift and has got slewed, and it is jammed betwixt the door and the ladder.' The man then thumped again upon the door, and cried to me, 'Are you alone?'

'Yes, I'm alone,' I answered.

'Keep up your heart; we'll soon have you out of it,' he cried. 'How long have you been locked up here? I cannot hear you. What! all night? Oh, my God! and a woman too, and alone!'

A distant voice sounded in a sort of halloa.

'This way,' cried the man outside my door. 'Bear a hand, my lads; here's a poor woman been locked up in this drowning brig all night.'

This was followed by some hearty English heave-ho's! and then a voice cried out, 'Jump for a handspike, Bill!' and several strange exclamations ensued, such as 'Heave, and raise the dead!' 'All together, now!' 'Another heave and the waggon's started!'

I heard a crash—the rolling of some heavy body—a strong English oath—and the door flew open.

Four men stood in the doorway in a group staring into the berth. One of them standing a little forward was a fine, tall, sailorly-looking young man of a ruddy complexion. He wore small whiskers, and was dressed plainly in a suit of pilot cloth with brass buttons, and around his naval cap were two thin bands of brass. The other three were 'common sailors,' as they are called, rough and sturdy fellows, any one of whom would have been a match for the whole of the four or five poor, half-starved French seamen who had formed the working part of the crew of the brig.

The young man with the brass upon his cap stared at me for some moments, as though dumbfounded with astonishment and pity.

'Well, well!' he cried, 'to think that if I'd been content to merely sing out to know whether anyone was aboard, I should have overlooked you!'

'Regular French job it seems, to leave a poor lady locked up alone down here arter this fashion,' exclaimed one of the sailors in a deep growling voice. 'Couldn't they have found time to have shoved that there cask out of the road of the door?'

The excitement of desperate emotions that had rendered my voice shrill beyond recognition of my own hearing had passed. The strange tranquillity which had visited my spirits during the night and possessed them throughout the awful hours had returned to me. Without agitation I extended my hand to the young officer, as I took him to be, and said to him in a quiet voice:

'Take me away. I have been locked up here all night.'

He took my hand and brought me into the living-room of the little brig.

'There is no hurry,' said he; 'this craft is going to make a good staunch derelict. I am here to find out if there is life to be saved. One of you men open the door of that berth there and overhaul it.'

My knees trembled and I sat down. The young mate ran his eye over the cabin, and, as though directed by peculiar oceanic instinct, walked to the locker in which Captain Regnier had been wont to keep a little stock of spirits and wine for present use, lifted the lid of the locker, and took out a bottle which he uncorked and applied to his nose.

'This will do,' said he. 'Simmonds, I noticed the scuttle-butt abreast of the main hatchway. Bring the dipper full of water here.'

This was done. The young officer mixed a glass of white spirits—gin or Hollands—and I drank. Then searching the locker afresh he found a biscuit which he handed to me. 'This will serve you,' he exclaimed, 'until we get you aboard, and then we will give you something warm and nourishing.' I ate a little of the biscuit, but it was dry as saw-dust and I swallowed with difficulty.

The three sailors stood at the table gazing at me, and their rough weather-darkened faces were full of sympathy and wonder. There was nothing to surprise me in their astonishment. My right brow and the upper part of my nose were still wrapped up with sticking plaister. Over my head was drawn the hood of mate Hénin's cloak, and the skirts of this ample garment enveloped me. My snow-white hair was disordered, and tresses of it fell past my ears on to my shoulders. And then I might also suppose that the agony of the night had wrought in my countenance and made of my face even a stranger mask than that which had looked out upon me from the handglass which the young Frenchman had held before it.

'Can you tell me,' asked the young officer, 'how many people were in this brig last night?'

I reflected and gave him the number.

'There is no doubt,' said he, earnestly looking about him and making a step to peer into the berth which had been occupied by Alphonse, and which one of the sailors had already examined, 'that all hands of the *men* took the boat and made off after the collision, leaving you, the only woman aboard, to sink or swim.'

'One of the Frenchmen tried to save me,' I answered; 'he had a good heart and would not have abandoned me, but he could not remove the cask, and his uncle, the captain, called to him to make haste and come on deck or they would leave him behind.'

'There are some berths yonder, aren't there?' said he, pointing to the forward wall where the sliding door with the ring was.

A seaman took the ring and slided the door open, and the three sailors passed through.

'Pray,' said the young officer, examining me with curiosity, 'might you have been the captain's wife?'

'No.'

He looked at my left hand. 'It was not to be expected,' he continued. 'I don't love the French, but I believe they don't make bad husbands. Were you a passenger in this vessel?'

I fixed my eyes upon the deck.

'Where was the brig bound to, can you tell me?'

'To Toulon.'

'From where?'

'From Boulogne-sur-Mer.'

He ran his eyes over me again but was interrupted in what he was about to say by the emergence of the three sailors.

'There's nothin' living to be seen,' said one of them.

'What *is* to be seen?' said the young mate.

'Vy, sir, in both cabins nautical instruments, charts, vearing apparel, Vellington boots, bedding, and de likes of such things as them.'

'We have rummaged the brig,' said the young officer; 'there's nothing left alive in her but this poor woman. Get the boat alongside, men. Are you strong enough,' said he, turning to me, 'to ascend those steps without aid?'

'I fear not,' I answered.

On this he put his arm around me and fairly carried me up the steps on to the deck.

When I was on deck I looked round. Many large clouds floated under the sky, and their shadows darkened the face of the ocean; but in the east was a corner of misty sun with an atmosphere of rose betwixt it and the sea-line, and a delicate pink glittered on the brows of the swell as the dusky green folds rolled to the risen luminary. The brig was a complete wreck. I could not believe that I was on board the same vessel that had rescued me. There was a great rift in her deck high above the water, though she sometimes rolled the black chasm dangerously close to the sea. Many feet of her bulwarks on the left-hand side were smashed into splinters. Her top-masts were broken, and they were washing at her side, held by lengths of rope which resembled eels of inordinate length crawling overboard. The white boat that used to stand in the fore part of the deck was gone, and the sort of sentry-box in which the food had been cooked was beaten into pieces. The hull was indeed the most perfect figure of a wreck that the imagination could conceive.

'A pretty collision, certainly!' said the young mate; 'but these dirty old coasting foreigners never will show a light.'

At the distance of about a quarter of a mile was a large ship. She was a far more beautiful vessel than the ship which had passed the brig, admirably graceful, swelling and swanlike as I had thought her. She was a long black ship, her sides as glossy as the hide of a well curried Arabian steed. So mirror-like was her length that the light that was upon the water trembled in cloudy flames in her sides. There was a radiant device of gold under the white bowsprit, and a line of gilt ran under the bulwarks from the radiant device to her stern, that likewise flamed with decorations in gilt. Her masts were white, and she had several white boats hanging at the extremities of curved iron bars at her sides. Some of the sails were pointed one way and some another, that one set might neutralise the impulse of the rest, and the noble and swelling and queenly ship lay without progress, softly leaning and gently bowing upon the swell whilst her spaces of canvas of a cream white softness showed like a large summer cloud against the shadowed sky of the horizon. She was close enough to enable me to distinguish a few figures moving about her, both in her fore and in her after parts.

'Oh! what is that ship?' I cried eagerly, the instant I saw her.

'She is the *Deal Castle*,' answered the young officer. 'She is the vessel that was in collision with this brig last night. After the collision we hove to, for there was nothing to be seen, and therefore nothing to be done. It was blowing fresh. We burnt a flare and sent up rockets, but nothing came of them. If the Frenchmen after launching their boat were not drowned they must have been blown away to a distance that lost them the sight of our rockets. Probably they were picked up in the small hours. There was nothing to be seen of their boat at daybreak this morning from yonder mastheads.'

He stepped to the side of the brig where the bulwarks were crushed, looked over, and then turning to me called out: 'Come along, if you please.'

I approached him, and looking down saw a large handsome white boat with five sailors in her, rising and falling at the side of the wreck.

'Stand by to catch hold of the lady,' exclaimed the young officer, and he lifted me over the edge of the wreck into the powerful grasp of a couple of sailors who received and seated me. In a few moments he had placed himself at the helm, and the seamen were rowing the boat to the ship.

I turned my eyes to view the receding brig. How miserable, how forlorn she looked! The great gap in her side resembled a frightful wound, and the *pouring* look of the black rigging streaming overboard made the ropes look like her life-blood draining from her heart into the ocean. I thought of the little berth in the hinder part of her, of the lantern that might still be dimly burning, of the disk of glass changing with soul-killing slowness from ebony into dim green, and from dim green into the yellow of daylight, and a sick shudder ran through my frame and I averted my head, and for a little while held my eyes closed.

'I should think,' said the young mate, clearly guessing what was passing in my mind, 'that your escape will be the narrowest on record.'

'I shall remember that I owe my life to you,' I answered, keeping my gaze downwards bent; for now the morning light had grown strong, and I could not bear that my face should be seen. I hung my head and raised my hand to the hood of the cloak, but the hood was as far forward as it would sit. However, the distance to be measured was short; the boat was swept along by the vigorous strokes of the seamen, and the young officer was too busy in manœuvring to run alongside the leaning and heaving ship to address or to heed me.

I perceived a group of some eight or ten people standing at the open rail which protected the edge of the raised deck in the sternmost portion of the ship. Their gaze was intently fixed upon us as we approached. Some of them were ladies. Along the line of the ship's bulwarks were many heads watching us. A tall man in a frock coat with brass buttons, detaching himself from the group in the after part, called to the young officer, who replied; but their speech was in the language of the sea, and I did not understand it. But even as we approached, a ladder was dropped over the ship's side; the young officer mounted, and then extended his hands to assist me up the steps, and very quickly I was transferred from the boat on to the deck of the ship.

I was left for some minutes alone; for, after the young mate had helped me to climb on board, he descended a ladder that conducted to the raised deck, on which were several ladies and gentlemen, and, touching his cap to the tall man in the uniform frock coat, he entered into conversation, both of them looking towards me as they talked. A large number of persons of both sexes—sixty or seventy in all, I dare say—thronged that part of the deck where I had entered the ship, and whilst I stood alone they gathered close about me, staring and whispering. They were of the emigrant class, the bulk of them rudely and poorly attired. A tawny-coloured woman, with braided black hair and eyes of an Egyptian duskiness, after staring at me awhile, exclaimed, 'Delicate Jesus, what a face! Shall I tell the sweet lady's fortune? And, gorgeous angels! look how her head is bound up.'

'Hold yer tongue!' cried a huge red-headed Irish woman, who had been surveying me with her arms akimbo. 'Pace ye haythen!' she exclaimed, letting fall her arms and talking with her hands clasped in a posture of supplication, 'can't ye tell who she is? She's a sister of mercy, and I know the order she belongs to. Sister, d'ye spake English? If you spake nothing but French, then give me your blessin' in French. Pull out the blessed crucifix from the pocket in which you have hidden it that ye mightn't lose it in the dreadful shipwreck, and bless me. I haven't heard a prayer since I've been on board. Oh! sake the place for a howly minute only of his sainted riverence, Father Murphy, me confessor that I shall never see again—oh, that I shall never see again!—and bless me.'

She spoke loudly, but in the most wailing voice that can be imagined, and when she ceased there was a sort of thrusting and shoving of a number of men and women to get near me, as though, poor souls! they desired to participate with the tall, red-haired virago in the prayer she had asked me to pronounce.

But whilst I stood surveying the rough and eager faces with alarm, the young mate came from the upper deck and said, 'Will you please step this way?'

I followed him into the saloon—a long, narrow, brilliant interior with several tables ranged down the centre of it. A number of stewards were engaged in preparing the tables for breakfast. There were two or three skylights, like domes, overhead, and there were many mirrors and plated lamps, and globes in which gold and silver fish were swimming, and rows of pots containing ferns. It was like passing from a cottage into a castle to exchange the living room of the little French brig for the comfort and splendour of the saloon of this noble ship.

CHAPTER VII
CAPTAIN FREDERICK LADMORE

A RESPECTABLE-LOOKING, pale-faced woman, attired in black, stood at the head of a staircase that descended through a large hatch in the forward part of this saloon. The young officer went up to her and said, 'Mrs. Richards, we have just brought this poor lady off from the brig that was run down last night. The captain requests that you will take her below and make her comfortable. She has been locked up—think of it, Mrs. Richards—she has been locked up all night, without food or drink, in the berth of a craft that I dare say she supposed at any moment might sink under her feet. When you have thoroughly refreshed yourself,' he exclaimed, addressing me, 'the captain will be happy to see you.'

'I think you had better come to my berth,' said the person whom the young mate had called Mrs. Richards.

'May I ask who you are?' said I.

'I am the stewardess,' she answered.

She then conducted me down the stairs into what I afterwards learnt was called the steerage. It was a part of the ship that corresponded with the saloon, only it was not so broad, and there were but two tables in the central passage or corridor. As in the saloon so here, there were berths or sleeping compartments ranged on either hand, but these quarters compared with the saloon were gloomy, and I do not remember how daylight was obtained to illuminate the place; yet one could see fairly well even when fresh from the glare of the deck.

The stewardess, opening a cabin door at the after end of the wide passage, bade me step in, and I found myself in a plain but comfortable little cabin, lighted by a large porthole, and furnished with two mahogany sleeping shelves one above the other. Upon a table were one or two account-books and a number of papers on files.

'Please to sit down, ma'm,' said the stewardess, speaking kindly. 'You look very weak and ill. Only fancy being locked up all night in that sinking boat! You are English?—— Yes, the third officer addressed you in English, and yet you may be French.

Let me help you to take off that heavy cloak. It is a man's cloak and a handsome one, I declare. I suppose you snatched at the first thing you could see to wrap yourself up in when our ship struck yours?'

She paused in her speech to hang up the cloak, and then surveyed me for a few moments in silence. I particularly observed that she ran her eye with an expression of surprise over my figure, as though she could not reconcile my white hair and withered face with my youthful shape. You will not require me to tell you that I was dressed in the plain, tight-fitting serge costume that I had worn when I made my last excursion with the boatman Hitchens. It had not suffered much from exposure, nor from the rude wear to which it had been subjected. It looked fairly fresh, and at any time I should have thought it still a wearable, serviceable dress.

'You appear to have hurt your head very badly,' said the stewardess. 'But the injury does not seem fresh—the plaister is surely older than last night?'

'Oh yes,' I answered.

'But questioning you is not carrying out the captain's orders, is it?' said she cheerfully. 'Now what shall I get you? What could you fancy? Would you like a plate of chicken and ham and a fresh crisp roll hot from the oven and a cup of hot coffee?'

I thanked her. She then pointed to a little fixed washstand in the corner, and told me to make use of her hair-brushes and whatever else I might require, and she then left me.

A square looking-glass hung over the washstand. I approached and looked into it and then shrunk from it. Oh! I could not wonder that the people in this ship had stared when I came on board. My white hair that had been thinned by every application of the brush fell raggedly down my back and upon my shoulders. My sallow complexion was rendered peculiarly sickly by the pallor that had been put into it by my sufferings during the night. The plaister was no longer white, but soiled, and when for the second time I looked at my face, I again shrank back and the old blind cry of my heart, *Who am I?* rose dumbly to my lips.

I sank trembling into a chair, and the words 'Oh God!' broke from me. But the word 'God' was no more than the echo of a sound, whose meaning was eclipsed. Again and again, and yet again, in my agony I had uttered that holy Name, but with no more sense of the meaning than the babe has when its tiny lips frame the syllables 'ma-ma.'

After waiting a little I poured out some water and washed my hands and face, and I then brushed my hair, but I observed that not so many hairs came away in the bristles as heretofore. I seated myself again and looked around me, and with kindling interest at the little furniture in the stewardess's berth. Near me hung a framed photograph of two children, a boy and a girl, and close by it hung another photograph of a respectably-dressed young woman in a bonnet, with an infant of a few months old on her knee. At these things I stared, and there followed an inward struggle that made me frown as I looked, and bite my lip and pluck at my dress with my fingers.

There were other photographs of grown-up people. I glanced at them, and at a little row of books, and at a work-basket, and at similar trivial details. But my eyes went quickly back to the portraits of the two children and the little baby, and I was still gazing at them when the stewardess entered, bearing my breakfast.

'Who are those children?' I asked her.

'My little nephew and niece,' she answered, smiling and lighting up as she spoke, 'and that is my only sister with her first-born on her lap. Oh, such a little cherub as it is! The sweetest baby! One, only one did I have. He was sweeter, yes, even sweeter than that child,' she added, her gaze lingering upon the photograph whilst her voice fell and her face grew grave. 'I lost him three months after my husband died——after he died and left me to —— to ——. But here is your breakfast now. Make a good meal. I am sure you need it.'

How much I needed it I did not know until I began to eat. I ate in silence, and the stewardess did not interrupt me by speech. She moved here and there, but all the while I was sensible that she eyed me furtively. When I had finished she said:

'Do you feel equal to seeing the captain? Or would you rather lie down and take some rest? You look as if you needed a long sleep.'

'Is the captain waiting to see me?' I asked.

She drew out her watch. 'He wishes to see you after breakfast, and the passengers will assemble at breakfast in a few minutes. Unless you feel very exhausted it might be as well that you should see him before you lie down. He will want to know where you come from, so as to be able to send you to your friends at the first opportunity. And then again you will wish to see the doctor? You must have been badly hurt to need so many straps about your head.'

'I do not feel exhausted,' I answered. 'This meal has greatly strengthened and refreshed me. I will sit here, if you please, until the captain is ready to see me.'

'I shall not be able to sit with you,' said the stewardess. 'My hands are very full. We are not long from port, and some of my ladies have not yet overcome their sea-sickness. And then I have a sweet, poor young lady to see after. She is very ill of consumption. I fear she will not live. Her mother is taking her on a voyage round the world, but, like most people who are ill of consumption, the young lady has started too late. At least, I fear so. I have seen too many instances in my time not to fear so.'

'Will you tell me,' said I, 'where this ship is going to?'

'To Sydney,' said she, pausing with her hand upon the door. She continued to watch me for a few moments, and then with a smile said, 'You know where Sydney is?' I held my eyes bent downwards. 'It is in Australia,' said she; 'in New South Wales. It is a beautiful city, and most people think that its harbour is the loveliest in the world.'

She opened the door, gave me a friendly nod, and passed out.

I remained seated, lost in such recent and slender thought as my mind could find to deal with. The ship was moving through the water. I could tell that by the tremble and hurry of light on the thick glass of the closed port. The movement was regular, buoyant, and wonderfully easy after the convulsive motions of the little brig. There was a clatter of crockery and subdued noise of talk outside in the somewhat darksome corridor, as I may call it, where some people—those no doubt who lodged in this part of the ship—were at breakfast. A baby was faintly crying in an adjacent cabin, but the compartments were stoutly divided, and every note reached the ear dimly. I sat thinking, and I thought of the terrible night I had passed, and of my abandonment by the young Frenchman and his companions, and also of the kind treatment I had met with on board the little French brig, and I thought of the days I had spent in her, and how the young Frenchman had said they had found me lying insensible, wounded, and bleeding in a boat with two masts; and, one thought leading to another, I suddenly arose and stepped to the looking-glass and gazed into it, and whilst I was staring at myself the door opened and the stewardess entered.

'I have just left the captain,' said she, 'and he will be glad to see you in his cabin if you are equal to the visit.'

'There are people about,' I answered; 'my face is—this plaister——' I put my hand to my brow, at a loss to express myself. I was ashamed to be seen, yet I was not able to say so.

'You look nicely—oh, you look nicely!' exclaimed the stewardess cordially. 'Consider what you have gone through. How many would look so well after being wounded as you have, and then locked up in a cabin all night in a sinking ship? But you will not be seen. There is a staircase at the end of this steerage, and it opens close against the cabin door. Come, dear lady!'

She was about to lead the way out when she stopped and said, 'What name shall I give when I show you in?'

'I do not know,' I answered.

She stared and looked frightened.

'I have lost my memory,' I said, and as I pronounced the words, I clasped my hands and bowed my head and sobbed.

'Ah, poor lady! God keep your heart! You have passed through a great deal surely,' said the kindly creature instantly, with a woman's sympathetic perception, witnessing the truth of my assurance and understanding my condition, and, tenderly taking my arm in her hand, she conducted me out of the berth.

She led me to a narrow staircase at the end of the corridor. I heard the voice of people at breakfast at the tables behind me, but I held my head bowed and saw nothing. We mounted the staircase and emerged at the aftermost end of the brilliant saloon, that was filled with the hum and busy with the clinking and clattering noises of passengers talking and lingering at the breakfast table. The stewardess knocked on the cabin door, and without waiting for a reply opened it, and we entered.

Two gentlemen arose from their chairs as I stepped in, and the stewardess, going up to one of them, said quickly but audibly, 'She has lost her memory, sir,' and so saying went out, giving me a smile as she passed.

The cabin into which I had been introduced was large and cheerful. It was furnished as a private sitting-room. On a table were a number of mathematical instruments; the deck was handsomely carpeted, and but for the movement to be felt, and but for one or two points of sea equipment, such as a silver telescope in a bracket and a sleeping-place or bunk that closed as though it were a horizontal cupboard, it would have been hard to imagine in this fresh, shining, comfortably furnished room that you were upon the ocean.

One of the gentlemen was the tall man who had been accosted by the young officer on our arrival. He was a very fine figure of a man indeed, above six feet tall and proportionately broad. His age was probably fifty, his complexion fresh, his eyes blue and kindly. There was but little of the look of the sailor, as we are taught by books to imagine him, in this man. With his grey whiskers, black-satin cravat, and dignified air, he might very well have passed for a well-to-do City banker or a country squire.

His companion on the other hand was a short man with sandy hair streaked with grey, and a dry, shrewd Scotch face. He was dressed in a suit of tweed, and I recollect that his boots resembled a pair of shovels, so square-toed were they.

'I am happy,' said the tall gentleman, in a slow, mild voice, after glancing at me with a mingled expression of pity and anxiety, 'to have been the instrument of delivering you from a terrible fate.' He placed a chair for me. 'Pray be seated. My name is Ladmore—Captain Frederick Ladmore, and I am in command of this ship, the *Deal Castle*. This gentleman is Mr. McEwan, the ship's surgeon.'

'Who strapped your forehead up, may I ask?' said Mr. McEwan, in a strong accent incommunicable by the pen, and he came close to me and stared at the plaister.

'A young Frenchman who belonged to the vessel from which you rescued me,' I answered.

'And a young 'un he must have been,' said Mr. McEwan, with a smile which disclosed gums containing scarcely more than four front teeth. 'How did he lay those strips on, ma'm? With a trowel?'

'You seem to have been badly hurt,' said Captain Ladmore compassionately.

'No, no, captain,' interrupted Mr. McEwan, 'never make too much of a woman's troubles or complaints. There's nothing to fret over unless the bridge of the nose be a trifle indented.'

'How did it happen?' inquired the captain.

'I was found in an open boat, lying insensible, with the mast of the boat across my face.'

'Oh! you were found in an open boat. By whom?' inquired the captain.

'By the people belonging to the French brig.'

'Now I understand,' said the captain. 'I thought you might have been—in fact, it puzzled me to know what you were doing on board that little craft. How long were you in the open boat?'

'I do not know.'

'What sort of boat was she?'

'I cannot remember.'

'But you surely remember how it happened that you were in that boat, and also how it happened that you were alone in her when rescued?'

'No, I do not remember,' I answered, biting my lip, whilst I was sensible that my inward struggle and agitation was causing me to frown.

The two gentlemen exchanged looks. 'I need not inquire whether you are English,' said the captain; 'your accent assures me on that head. And forgive me for saying that no one could hear you speak without being satisfied as to your station in life. Let me see if I can help your memory: you are a lady who in all probability engaged a pleasure boat to take a cruise in, and you were venturesome enough to go alone. The boat proved too much for you and she ran away with you. Or, dirty weather came on and blew you out of sight of land.'

I listened to him with my eyes fastened upon the deck, greedily devouring his speech; but all remained dark. I hearkened and I understood him, and I believed that it might be as he had said, but I could not say that it was so. No! no more indeed than had he been telling me the experience of another of whom I had never heard.

'In what part was your boat fallen in with?' he asked after a pause.

'I cannot tell.'

'How long were you on board the brig?'

This question I could answer. He rose and took a chart from a corner of the cabin, and then sat again with his finger upon the open chart.

'Concede an average of sixty miles a day to that brig,' said he, addressing Mr. McEwan. 'Her weather will have been ours, and we may take it that her average will not have exceeded sixty miles a day in the time during which the lady was aboard her.' His lips moved as he calculated to himself, and then, passing his finger over the chart, he said: 'The situation of the open boat when the French brig fell in with her would be about— —' and he indicated the place by stating the latitude and longitude of it.

'That'll be clear of the Chops, captain,' said Mr. McEwan, 'and at *that*, though the lady may hail from England, she never can have sailed from that country.'

'It certainly would be a prodigious drift for a small boat,' said the captain, looking at the chart and speaking in a musing way. 'It should signify a week's drift, unless the boat kept her stern to it with all sail set. Perhaps I do not allow enough for the brig's average run.'

'The lady may have been blown from a French port,' said Mr. McEwan.

'What French port?' inquired the captain, moving the chart that the surgeon might see it.

'I have an idea!' said Mr. McEwan; 'why must the lady have been blown from a port at all? And why should the boat in which she was discovered *necessarily* have been a pleasure-boat? Who's to say that she is not the sole survivor of some disastrous shipwreck? In that case she may have been coming home from the other side of the world. There's more happened to her, Captain Ladmore,' said he, speaking with his eyes fixed upon me, 'than is to be occasioned by misadventure during a pleasure cruise.'

'Cannot you describe the boat?' said the captain to me.

'The Frenchman told me that she was an open boat and that she had two masts,' I answered.

'Did they notice no more of her than that?'

'No. She was entangled with the rigging and drove along with the brig for a short distance. She broke away after I had been taken out of her, and the Frenchman let her go. It was a little before daybreak, and there was scarcely any light to see by.'

'You remember all that!' exclaimed Mr. McEwan.

'I remember everything that the Frenchman told me,' I answered; 'and I can remember everything that has happened from the hour of my returning to consciousness on board the brig.'

'Would not a ship's quarter-boat have two masts, captain?' said Mr. McEwan. 'Ye must know it is my theory that 'tis a case of shipwreck, and that this lady may be the only survivor. Who can tell?'

'I have known a ship's long-boat with two masts,' answered Captain Ladmore, 'but I never heard of a quarter-boat so rigged.'

'Then the boat that the Frenchman fell in with may have been a long-boat,' said the surgeon.

'I wish to find out all about you,' said the captain gravely and quietly, glancing at my bare hands and then running his eyes over my dress, 'that I may be able to send you home. A home you must have—but where? Cannot you tell me that it is in England?'

I looked at him, and my swimming eyes sank. I could not speak.

'This is sad indeed,' said he. 'Did you ever hear of so complete a failure of memory, McEwan?'

'Oh yes,' answered the surgeon. 'I'll show you fifty examples of utter failure in a book on the brain which I have in my cabin, and I can give you half a dozen instances at least out of my own experience. At the same time,' he continued, speaking as though I were not present, 'this case is peculiar and impressive. But I should regard it as hopeful on the whole because, ye see, there's the capacity of recollecting everything on this side of whatever it may be that occasioned the loss.'

'Did the Frenchman find nothing in the boat?' asked the captain gently.

'Nothing,' I replied, 'except a straw hat that was crushed by the fall of the mast, and stained by my wounds.'

'It was your hat?'

'They thought so,' I answered.

'Nothing more?' said he, 'merely a straw hat? But then to be sure it was in the dark of the morning, and they were able to see nothing more.'

He rose from his chair and took several turns about the cabin; meanwhile Mr. McEwan steadfastly regarded me. His air was one of professional curiosity. At last his scrutiny grew painful, but he did not relax it, though my uneasiness must have been clear to him.

'Can you give me any idea,' said the captain, 'of what became of the French crew?'

'I cannot,' I replied.

'It was barbarous of them to leave you on board a vessel which they believed was sinking, or they would not have quitted her.'

'I was kindly treated by them,' I answered. One of them, a young Frenchman, endeavoured to release me that I might gain the deck. But he could not move the cask that was jammed between my door and the steps. His uncle, the captain, threatened to leave him behind. The young man would have saved me could he have procured help.'

'That's how it always is in a panic at sea,' said the captain, addressing Mr. McEwan. 'I can tell you exactly how it happened with those foreigners. When the brig was struck the seamen supposed that she would instantly founder. They launched the boat, probably their only boat.'

'They had but one boat,' I said.

'Just so,' exclaimed the captain; 'they launched their only boat, and then as they lay alongside they shouted to their skipper that if he delayed they would leave him. No man has a chance with a cowardly crew at such a time. I dare say, had it depended upon the French captain and his nephew, you would have been brought on deck and taken into the boat. But well for you, poor lady, that they did not stay to release you! They blew away in the blackness, and in such a sea as was running it is fifty to one if the boat was not capsized.'

'Are there no initials upon your linen, ma'm?' inquired the surgeon.

I produced from my pocket the handkerchief which the young Frenchman had examined, and handed it to the surgeon, saying, 'This was in my pocket when I was rescued, and it must therefore be mine. The letters "A. C." are upon it. My underlinen is similarly marked.'

He looked at the initials, and then passed the handkerchief to the captain.

'Do not the letters suggest your name to you?' said the surgeon. I shook my head. 'Would you know your name if I were to pronounce it, d'ye think?'

'I cannot say.'

'Have you run over any names for yourself?'

'I cannot think of any names to run over,' said I.

'Ha!' exclaimed the captain, 'how great, how awful is the mystery of life, is the mystery of the mind!' and as though overcome he stepped to the porthole and seemed to look out, keeping his back upon us. Mr. McEwan continued to scrutinise me.

'Captain,' he suddenly exclaimed again, speaking as though I were deaf or absent, 'the lady's hair is snow white, d'ye mark? Her hair, as we see it, doesn't correspond with her figure. She's much younger than the colour of her hair. She is much younger than the look of her face, captain. She's a young woman that has been suddenly aged—to the sight. I can see the youth of her lurking under her countenance, like comely lineaments under a veil. As she recovers strength and health, her bloom will return.' He turned to me. 'When you entered the boat in which you were found insensible, your hair, m'am, was black.'

'But all this is not to the point, McEwan,' exclaimed the captain, coming from the porthole before which he had been standing with his back upon us. 'The question is, where does this lady live? Has she friends in England. If so, it is my duty to send her home by the first ship. But your memory,' said he to me, 'may return in a day or two, and we are not acting kindly in detaining you from the rest which I am sure you need after such a night as you have endured.'

He opened the door of his cabin, and called to one of the stewards to send Mrs. Richards to him.

'You'll forgive me, ma'm,' said Mr. McEwan, 'but I observe that you have no rings. Now I'm sure you must have had rings on when you were found in the boat. Were they stolen from you, d'ye think?'

I looked at my hands and answered, 'I was without rings when my consciousness returned.'

'A pity!' exclaimed the surgeon impatiently; 'there might be the clue we seek in a ring of yours. Have ye no jewellery?'

'I have nothing but this purse,' I answered, and I gave it to him.

'English money at all events, captain,' he cried, emptying the contents into his hand. 'But what does that tell? Merely that English money circulates everywhere.'

The stewardess entered.

'Mrs. Richards,' said Captain Ladmore, 'you will please prepare a berth for this lady in the steerage. See that she is made perfectly comfortable, and the conveniences which she stands in need of that the ship can supply let her have.'

'I do not know how to thank you,' I said in a broken voice.

'Not a word of thanks, if you please,' he answered. 'You have suffered sadly, and for no inconsiderable part of your suffering is this ship responsible. We must make you all the amends possible.'

He motioned to the stewardess who opened the door.

'I'll not worry you now with looking at your head and dressing it,' said Mr. McEwan; 'take some rest first. I'll call in upon you by-and-by.'

We passed into the brilliant saloon. The sun was now high, and his beams glittered gloriously upon the skylights, and were multiplied in a hundred sparkling prisms in the mirrors, lamps, and globes of fish. Through the windows of the skylight some of the sails of the ship were visible, and they rose swelling and towering and of a surf-like whiteness to the windy sky that lay in a hazy marble over the mastheads. The stewards were stripping the tables of the breakfast things, and at the forward end of the saloon stood a group of ladies conversing, and looking through a window on to the decks beyond, where a multitude of the emigrant or third-class passengers were assembled.

I held my head bowed, for I was ashamed to be seen. The stewardess took me to her berth, and when I had entered it I sat down, and putting my hands to my heart I rocked myself and tried to weep, for my heart felt swollen as though it would burst, and my head felt full, and my breathing was difficult; but the tears would not flow. Many hours of anguish had I passed since consciousness had returned to me on board the brig, but more exquisite than all those hours of anguish put together was the agony my spirit underwent as I sat in the stewardess's berth rocking myself. No light! no light! Oh, I had hoped for some faint illumination from the questions which had been asked me, from the sentences which the captain and the surgeon had exchanged about me. The blackness was as impenetrable as ever it had been. I groped with my inward vision over the thick dark curtain, but no glimmer of light crossed it, no fold stirred. The silence and the blackness were of the tomb. It was as though I had returned to life to find myself in a coffin, there to lie straining my eyes against the impenetrable darkness, and there, in the grave, to lie hearkening to the awful hush of death.

'Come, cheer up, dear,' said the stewardess, putting her hand upon my shoulder. 'Stay, I have something that will do you good,' and going to a shelf she took down a little decanter of cherry-brandy and gave me a glassful.

'They told me things that may be true, and I do not know whether they are true or not,' said I.

'What did they say, dear?'

'They said that I was young, and that my hair was black before I lost my memory; and they said that I might be the only survivor of a shipwreck, and that there was nothing—nothing—oh! *nothing* to tell where I came from, where my home was, what my name is——!

'Now you must have patience, and you must keep up your courage,' said the stewardess. 'Wait till you see poor Miss Lee. You will not think that yours is the greatest or the only trouble in this world. *She* is certainly dying, but you will not die, I hope. You will get strong, and then your memory will return, and you will go home, and the separation will not be long, you will find. It is not like dying. There is no return then,' said she, glancing at the photograph of the little baby on the woman's knee; 'and besides,' she continued, looking at my hand, 'whether you remember or not, you may be sure that you are not married, and, therefore, have no husband or children wondering what has become of you. You may, indeed, have a father and mother, and perhaps sisters, and others like that, but separation from *them* is not like separation from husband and children. So, dear, think how much worse it might be, and go on hoping for the best. And now I am going to prepare a berth for you, and get a bath ready. There is an empty berth next door, and you shall have it. And you shall also have what you sadly need, a comforting change of linen.'

She then left me.

An hour later I was lying, greatly refreshed, in the berth which the good-hearted Mrs. Richards had got ready for me. A warm salt-water bath had taken all the aching out of my limbs. No restorative could have proved so life-giving. It soothed me—Oh! the embrace and enfoldment of the warm, green, sparkling brine was deliciously grateful beyond all power of words after the long days which I had passed in my clothes—in clothes which the rain had soaked through to the skin, and which had dried upon me. When I had bathed, I replaced my underclothing by some clean linen lent to me by the stewardess. And when, having entered my new berth, I had brushed my hair and refreshed my face with some lavender water which Mrs. Richards had placed with brushes and other toilet articles upon a little table—when, having done this, I got into my bunk, or sleeping-shelf, and found myself resting upon a hair mattress, with a bolster and pillow of down for my head, I felt as though I had been born into a new life, as though some base and heavy burden of sordid physical pain and distress had been taken from me. My mind, too, was resting. The inward weary wrestling had ceased for a time. I lay watching the lines of golden sunlight rippling upon a circle of bluish splendour cast by the large circular porthole upon the polished chestnut-coloured bulkhead near the door, until my eyes closed and I slumbered.

CHAPTER VIII
A KIND LITTLE WOMAN

WHEN I awoke my gaze was directed at the face of Mr. McEwan, who stood at the side of my bedplace looking at me. The cabin was full of strong daylight, but the atmosphere was tinctured with a faint rose, and had I at that moment given the matter a thought, I should have known that I had slept far into the afternoon.

In spite of my eyes being open the ship's surgeon continued to view me without any change of posture or alteration of countenance. He might have been waiting to make sure that I was conscious; he scrutinised me, nevertheless, as though his eyes were gimlets, with which he could pierce into my brain. He held a volume in his hand, but on his appearing to make up his mind that I was awake he put the book into the bunk that was above me, and said, 'You sleep well.'

'I have slept well to-day,' I answered; 'I bathed and was much comforted before I lay down.'

'Do you ever dream?' he asked.

'Never.'

'Are you sure?'

'My memory on this side of my recovery is good,' I said; 'and if I dreamt I should recollect my dreams. I have longed with passion to dream, because I have a fancy that my memory may return to me in a vision.'

'That is not unlikely,' said he. He took the book from the upper bunk, drew a chair close to me, and seated himself.

'I have been looking at you in your sleep,' said he, 'and I am confirmed in my first opinion—you are a young woman. Your age is four- or five-and-twenty. You smiled shortly before you awoke, and your smile was like a light thrown upon your youth hidden behind your face. Some dream must have produced that smile—but the mere phantom of a phantom of a dream, too colourless and attenuated for your mind to recollect. And your hair! Has it been coming out of late?'

'I have lost a great quantity. It came out in handfuls, but it no longer falls as it did.'

'Your hair was black,' said he, smiling, 'and very abundant and fine. Before your calamity—whatever it might be—befell you you were a handsome young woman, excellently shaped, with dark, speaking eyes, and a noble growth of hair. Take my word for it. And now think. Do I give you any ideas?'

I shut my eyes to think, and I thought and thought, but to no purpose.

'No matter,' he exclaimed; 'do not strain your mind. Take things perfectly easy. I have been reading in several volumes I possess on cases resembling yours; and here is a book,' he continued, 'with some examples, two of which you shall hear, that you may take heart.'

He balanced a pair of gold glasses on his nose and read as follows, slowly and deliberately:—

'A young clergyman, when on the point of being married, suffered an injury of the head by which his understanding was entirely and permanently deranged. He lived in this condition till the age of eighty, and to the last talked of nothing but his approaching wedding, and expressed impatience of the arrival of the happy day.'

'What do you think of that?' said the surgeon.

I did not answer.

'Do you understand it?' said he.

'I understand it,' I replied, 'but I do not see what it has to do with the memory.'

'There is too much memory in it,' he exclaimed with a dry smile; 'but you are right, and I'm very well satisfied that you should be able to reason. Now I will read you something that *does* concern the memory, and you shall be consoled when you hear it;' and he read aloud as follows:—

'On her recovery from the torpor she appeared to have forgotten nearly all her previous knowledge: everything seemed new to her, and she did not recognise a single individual, not even her nearest relatives. In her behaviour she was restless and inattentive, but very lively and cheerful: she was delighted with everything she saw and heard, and altogether resembled a child more than a grown person. At first it was scarcely possible to engage her in conversation: in place of answering a question she repeated it aloud in the same words in which it was put. At first she had very few words. She often made one word answer for all others which were in any way allied to it: thus, in place of *tea* she would ask for *juice*. She once or twice had dreams, which she afterwards related to her friends, and she seemed quite aware of the difference betwixt a dream and a reality.'

'Now mark this,' continued the surgeon, looking at me over his glasses; and he then read:—

'After a time Mrs. H—— was able to return to her home in England, where she passed the rest of her life happily with her husband. She was in the habit of corresponding by letter with her friends at a distance, and lived on the most agreeable terms with her immediate neighbours, by whom she was held in much regard on account of her kindly nature and charitable work.'

'So you see,' said Mr. McEwan, 'that the poor thing got quite well.'

'Is that a good book?' said I, looking at it.

'It is a first-rate book,' he answered.

'But the woman's memory was not utterly gone, as mine is.'

'She was far worse than you,' said he. 'Be of good cheer. Think of your brain as a theatre. The curtain has come down with a run, and the gentleman whose business it is to wind it up is drunk, or absent through illness. We'll rout him out by-and-by, and the curtain will rise again. And now sit up, if you please, that I may look at your head.'

He was abrupt and off-hand in his speech, with something of the wag in him, but already was I sensible that there was an abundance of good-nature and of kindly feeling underlying his manner. He carefully renewed the plaister and examined the injured brow, then dressed it with some salve and bandaged it with a tender hand. I asked him if I was disfigured.

'An excellent question,' he explained; 'a woman's question. Go on asking every question that may occur to you; but do not strain your mind to recollect.'

'Am I disfigured?' I asked.

'That is right,' said he; 'go on questioning me.'

'Let me look at the glass.'

'No; don't you see that I am about to bandage you—so! Do not remove this bandage. There is something that needs to heal, and your young Frenchman's sticking-plaister has not helped you.'

The surgeon left me after saying that he would send me a powerful tonic, which I was to take so many times a day, and when he was gone I got out of the bunk, in which I had slept fully dressed, and going to the glass over the washstand looked into it. The face that gazed back upon me was no longer the forbidding, the almost repulsive countenance that I remembered. The removal of the darkened and bloodstained strips of sticking-plaister had made a wonderful difference. In their place was a snow-white bandage, skilfully fitted. It hid a portion of the right brow, and descended so as to conceal the bridge of the nose, but it left my right eye visible; and when I looked at my eyes I observed that they were no longer leaden and lustreless, but that, on the contrary, there was the light of life in them, and the dark pupils soft and liquid.

This I knew by comparing my face with the face with which I had awoke to consciousness on board the brig; but I remembered no other face than *that*.

I stood for some while staring in the glass, recalling the assurance of the surgeon that I was a woman of four- or five-and-twenty, and contrasting that notion with the belief Alphonse had expressed, that my age was forty-five, and I kept on saying to myself, *Who am I?* and silently repeating over and over again the letters A. C. until, recalling Mr. McEwan's advice to me not to strain my brain, I broke away with a sudden horror, as of insanity, from the glass, and went to the cabin porthole.

I could see very little of the sky and sea, but what I saw was beautiful with the colouring of the rich dark gold of sunset. I gazed almost directly west, and as much as I could behold of the heavens that way was a glowing and a throbbing crimson, barred with streaks of violet gloriously edged with ruby flames. The sea ran red as the sky; every ridged head of purple broke into rosy froth. In the heart of this little circle of western magnificence formed by the porthole was a ship with orange-coloured sails. I watched her, and thought of the young Frenchman, and wondered whether the crew of the brig had perished, as Captain Ladmore supposed, or whether they had been picked up during the darkness of the night by some vessel that had passed at too great a distance to be observed by the people of the *Deal Castle*.

Whilst I stood thus looking and thinking, the door was opened by an under-steward to enable Mrs. Richards to enter with a tray, which she grasped with both hands.

'I thought,' said she, smiling as she placed the tray full of good things upon the deck, 'that you would rather have your tea here than at the table outside, and with your leave I will drink a cup of tea with you. Ah! now you look better. Yes, your eyes have cleared wonderfully; and I don't see the same expression of pain in your face. And how much better that bandage looks than the ugly sticking-plaister.'

She chatted thus whilst she gazed around, considering how she should dispose of the tray. At last she placed it in my bed, where it would be safe—where, at least, it would not slide, for there was a heave running from the sunset through the sea, and the ship regularly leaned upon it, but in motions so stately as scarcely to be noticeable. We seated ourselves by the side of the bed and ate and drank. She had brought cold fowl, and ham-and-tongue, and pressed beef, and fancy rolls of bread, all which, with other things, after the fare I had been used to on board the brig, were true dainties and delicacies to me, and particularly did I enjoy the tea with its dash of new milk.

'I had some trouble,' said the stewardess, looking into the milk-jug, 'to coax this drop out of the steward. There is but one cow, and there are many demands upon poor Crummie. But I felt sure you would enjoy a cup of tea with milk in it.'

She then asked me what Mr. McEwan had said, and I told her.

'He is a clever man, I believe,' said she.

'Oh, if he would only give me back my memory!' I exclaimed.

'I wonder what the captain means to do with you,' said she.

'And I, too, wonder. Have I a home? Surely I must have a home somewhere? It cannot be that I am utterly alone in the world, though I am so now.'

'No, dear, you will not be alone. God will raise up friends for you until He gives you back your memory; and then——'

'But this ship is going on a long voyage,' said I, 'and if I remain in her she will be carrying me away from where my home may be.'

'Yes, but if your home is in England, this ship will convey you back there if you remain in her.'

'How long will it take the ship to sail to the place you spoke of?'

'Sydney. She is going to Sydney. Well, it may take her three months, or it may take her four months, to get there, and she will stop at Sydney for three months. We all hope—all of us, I mean, whose homes are in England—to be home by next August.'

I turned her words over in my mind, but was unable to attach any meaning to what she said. I could not understand *time*— that is, I did not know what Mrs. Richards meant when she spoke of 'next August.' But I would not question her; my incapacity made me feel ashamed, and exquisitely wretched at heart, and I asked no questions, lest she should divine that I did not comprehend her.

There were people drinking tea at the tables outside. I heard the occasional cry of a baby, the voices of children, the murmur of men and women conversing. Mrs. Richards informed me that those people were second-class passengers, who inhabited this part of the ship.

'Are there many passengers in all?' I asked.

'Oh yes, the ship is full of men and women,' she replied.

'Where do they come from?'

'The ship sailed from London. The people joined her at the docks, or at Gravesend, from all parts of the kingdom.'

'Oh,' cried I, clasping my hands, 'if there were but a single person amongst the crowds on board—a single person who knew me, who would be able to pronounce my name and tell me where my home is—if, indeed, I have a home!'

'Well, who knows but there may be such a person?' said the stewardess. 'Big as this world is, we are constantly running against friends or acquaintances. Everybody is asking after you. All my ladies, all the people I attend on, make inquiries after you every time I see them. There is a dear old lady on board, Mrs. Lee; she is the mother of the poor consumptive girl. Not half an hour ago, as I was passing through the saloon, Mrs. Lee left her chair and said to me, "Mrs. Richards, if there is anything that I or my daughter can do for the poor lady who was rescued this morning, I beg you will enable us to serve her. I fear she is without clothes," said Mrs. Lee. "How could it be otherwise, indeed? Now my daughter and I have plenty of clothes, and the poor lady is welcome to whatever she wants."'

'How good of her!' I exclaimed. 'Thank her, thank her for me, Mrs. Richards.'

'She is a dear old lady, and her daughter is the sweetest of girls. Oh dear! oh dear! that the hand of Death should be drawing closer and closer to steal away so much beauty and gentleness.'

'Is it known that—that——'

'That you have lost your memory?'

I sank my head.

'Why, yes. News flies fast on board ship. And why should it not be known? Your not having your memory will explain a great deal.'

'What will it explain?'

'For instance, your having no name.'

'My initials are A. C.,' said I, and I pronounced the letters several times over, and cried out, 'What can they stand for?'

'But would you know your name if you saw it?' said the stewardess.

'I cannot tell.'

As I made this answer the door was quietly rapped. 'Come in,' said the stewardess, and the captain entered. The stewardess rose, and stood as though a royal personage had walked in, and then made a step to the door.

'Do not go away, Mrs. Richards,' cried Captain Ladmore. 'I am glad to see that you are carefully attending to the lady'—and he asked me if I felt better.

I answered that I felt very much better, and that I did not know how to express the gratitude which all the kindness I had received and was receiving had filled my heart with. He pulled a chair and seated himself near me.

'I have been all day,' said he with a grave smile, 'considering what course to adopt as regards your disposal. I should very well know what to do if you could give me any hint as to where you come from.' He paused, as though hoping I might now be able to give him such a hint. He then continued: 'In my own mind I have little doubt that you are English, and that your home is in England. But I cannot be quite sure of this, and I should wish to be convinced before acting. At any hour, whether to-morrow or the following day—at any hour we may fall in with a ship bound to England whose captain might be willing to receive you and to land you. But then, unless your memory returns during the homeward run, what would a captain be able to do with you when he reached port? He would land you—yes; but humanity would not suffer him to let you leave his ship without your memory, without possessing a friend to go to, and, pardon me for adding, with only a few shillings in your pocket.'

I hid my face and sobbed.

'Don't take on, dear,' said Mrs. Richards, gently clasping my wrist; 'wait a little till you hear what the captain has to say. Yours is a sorrowful, sad case, and it has to be thought over,' and here her voice failed her.

'A bad disaster,' continued the captain, 'has brought you into my ship and placed you under my care. I am obliged to put your own situation and condition to you fairly and intelligibly. If your home is in England, I should not wish to keep you on board my ship and carry you to Australia. But your home may not be in England, and I dislike the thought of sending you to that country, where, for all I know, you may have no friends. When your memory returns we shall gather exactly how to act.'

'I do not seem able to think, I do not feel able to reason,' I exclaimed, putting my hand to my forehead.

'Do not trouble to think or to reason either,' said the stewardess; 'the captain will do it for you.'

'What,' said Captain Ladmore, fixing his eyes upon Mrs. Richards, but talking as though he thought aloud—'what should I be able to tell the shipmaster to whom I transferred this lady? I should have positively nothing whatever to tell him. He might hesitate to receive her. His reluctance would be justified. I myself should certainly hesitate to receive a shipwrecked lady under such circumstances. I should say to myself, When I arrive, whom shall I find to receive her? There might, indeed, be philanthropic institutions to take her in, but if I could not find such an institution, what should I do? I should have to take charge of her until I could place her somewhere. I might, indeed, advertise, send a letter to the newspapers, and trust by publishing her case to make her existence known to her friends. But then she may have no friends in England—and meanwhile? I have thought the matter over,' said he, addressing me, 'and believe that I cannot do better than keep you on board, with a chance of your memory returning at any moment, and enabling me *then* to take the first opportuning of sending you to your home, wherever it may be. What do you think?'

'I cannot think. Oh, if but the dimmest idea would visit my mind to help you and to help me! It would be dreadful,' I said in a voice that was failing me, 'to find myself on shore, in destitution, without friends, not knowing what to do, where to go. *That* thought was a horror to me in the French brig, when the Frenchmen talked of landing me at Toulon and handing me over to the British Consul. I remember what they said: What would the British Consul do for me?' And then I sprang from my chair and cried out, hysterically, 'Oh, Captain Ladmore, what is to become of me? what is to become of me?'

'You are amongst friends. Do not take on so, dear,' said the stewardess.

'It is my dreadful loneliness,' I cried, speaking out of the old terror that was again upon me—the miserable terror that had possessed me again and again on board the Frenchman.

'All of us are alone,' said the captain, in his deep, serious voice; 'we arrive and we depart in loneliness. God Himself is alone.'

'Think of that!' said the stewardess.

'Whilst you are with us,' said Captain Ladmore, 'it is proper that you should be known by some name. Your initials are clearly A. C. Now suppose we call you Miss C.? By so terming you we shall be preserving as much of your real name as we can discover.' He paused, and a moment later added, addressing the stewardess, 'Do you suggest Miss C. or Mrs. C., Mrs. Richards?'

'Oh! Miss C., sir, undoubtedly,' she answered.

I lifted my head, and perceived the captain examining me as scrutinisingly as the western light that was now weak and fast waning would permit.

'Then Miss C.,' said he, rising slowly, and smiling gravely as he pronounced the name, 'you will consider yourself the guest of the ship *Deal Castle* for the present. By-and-by your memory will return to you. We shall then learn all about you, and *then*, whatever steps I take must certainly result in restoring you to your friends; whereas to tranship you now—— But that is settled,' he added, with a dignified motion of the hand.

He pulled out his watch, held it to the porthole, and then bidding the stewardess see that I wanted for nothing, gave me a bow and went out. Mrs. Richards produced a box of matches from her pocket, and lighted a bracket lamp.

'What do you think of Captain Ladmore?' she asked.

'He is the soul of goodness, Mrs. Richards.'

'He is, indeed. Who would suppose him to be a sea-captain? Sea-captains are thought to be a very rough body of men. Before I come upon the water as a stewardess I used to imagine all sea-captains as persons with red faces wrinkled like walnut-shells, and boozy eyes. They all had bandy legs, and used bad language. Since then I have met many sea-captains, and some of them are as I used to think they all were; but some are otherwise, and Captain Ladmore is one of them. On his return home two or three voyages ago he found his wife and only daughter dead. They had died while he was away. The blow was dreadful. He cannot forget it, they say. It changed his nature—it made him a sad, grave man, and thus he will always be. Well, now I must go and attend to my work.'

I opened the door, and she passed out bearing the tray.

The floating swing of the ship was so steady that I was able to walk about my cabin with comfort. I paced round and round it with my hands clasped behind me and my eyes fixed on the floor, thinking over what Captain Ladmore had said. On the whole I was comforted. It startled me, it shocked me, indeed, when I thought that unless my memory returned I was to be carried all the way to Australia. Not that I had any clear ideas as to where Australia was, or its distance from the ship, and, as I have before said, I was unable to grasp the meaning of time as conveyed by the stewardess's information that the passage out would occupy three months or four months as it might be. But from what Mr. McEwan and Captain Ladmore and Mrs. Richards had said among them, I could in some manner understand that Sydney, whither the ship was bound, was an immense distance off, and though I had not the least idea where my home was—whether it was in England or in America, as the young Frenchman had suggested, or in that very continent of Australia to which the *Deal Castle* was voyaging—yet the mere notion of being carried a vast distance, and for no other purpose than to give my memory time to revive, with the certainty, moreover, that if my memory had not returned to me at the end of the voyage I should be as lonely, miserable, and helpless as I now was: here were considerations, as I say, to startle and shock me.

But on the whole I felt comforted. It was the prospect of being set ashore friendless at Toulon that had immeasurably added to my wretchedness whilst on board the Frenchman. But now that threatened state of hopelessness, of poverty, of homelessness, all to be exquisitely complicated by total mental blindness, was indefinitely postponed or removed. I had met with people who were taking pity on me, and amongst whom I might find friends. My health, too, would now be professionally watched. And then, again, if my home *were* in England, this ship would certainly in time return to that country, and in the long weeks between it might be that my memory would be restored to me. Therefore, as I walked about in my cabin I felt on the whole comforted.

Mrs. Richards brought me an armful of books, some of her own, and some from the ship's little collection. She said, as she put the volumes down—it was about seven o'clock in the evening:—

'Do you feel dull? If so, there are many in the saloon who would be glad to meet you and converse with you.'

'No, I am not dull. My mind is much more tranquil than it was. I am thinking of last night. How glad I am to be here!'

'Would you like to receive a visit? There are many who would be delighted to visit you. Mrs. Lee will gladly come and sit with you if you feel strong enough for a chat.'

'I would rather remain quiet, Mrs. Richards. To-morrow I hope—— Perhaps in a day or two the doctor will remove this bandage.'

'You must not think of your appearance,' she said, smiling, 'although it is a good sign. A little vanity is always a good sign in invalids. I would not give much for the life of an invalid woman who is without a touch of womanly conceit. But you are very well; you look very nicely. Do not think of your bandage,' and with a kindly smile and nod she left me.

When I went to bed I found myself sleepless. But sleeplessness I might have expected after my deep slumbers during the day. At nine o'clock Mrs. Richards had brought me some brandy-and-water and biscuits, and when she left me I went to bed, and lay listening to the people in the steerage outside. I gathered that some of them were playing at cards: there were frequent short exclamations, and now and again a noisy peal of laughter. The sea was smooth and the ship was going along quietly; no creaking, no sounds of straining vexed the quiet when a hush fell upon the players.

At ten o'clock there was a tap upon my door, and the voice of a man bade me put my light out. I extinguished the lamp and returned to my bed. All was silent outside now; nothing was to be heard save a dim swarming noise of broken waters hurrying by, and at intervals the cry of a baby. For some time I listened to this cry, and it produced not the least effect upon me; but suddenly, on my hearing it more clearly, as though the door of the cabin in which the infant lay had been opened, a feeling of dreadful grief seized me—a feeling of dreadful loneliness. I sat up in my bed and racked my mind—I know not how else to express what I felt in my effort to *compel* my mind to seek in the black void of memory for the reasons why that infant's cry had raised in me so insufferable a sense of grief, so incommunicable an ache of loneliness.

I grew calm and closed my eyes, but I could not sleep. Time passed, and still finding myself sleepless, I quitted my bed and went to the porthole, and perceived through the glass the bluish haze of moonlit darkness, with many brilliant stars in it, rhythmically sliding to the movements of the ship. I cannot sleep, I said to myself. I slept too deeply to-day to slumber now; I will go on deck. The fresh air will revive me. It is dreadful to be in this gloom, alone and bitterly wakeful, thinking of this time last night.

So I put on my clothes—sheen enough flowed through the porthole to see by—and I took from a peg on the door the cloak in which I had been wrapped when I left the brig, and enveloped myself in it, pulling the hood over my head, and quietly stepped out. I remembered that there was a ladder at either end of the steerage, and that the deck was the more easily to be gained by the foremost ladder. A lamp burnt at one end of the steerage, and with the help of its rays I easily made my way to the foot of the steps. All was buried in deep silence. I mounted the steps and gained the foremost end of the saloon, and silently opening a door I passed out on to the quarterdeck, into the windy, moonlit, starry night.

END OF THE FIRST VOLUME